Your Fi
100 Days

FT Prentice Hall
FINANCIAL TIMES

In an increasingly competitive world, we believe it's quality of thinking that gives you the edge – an idea that opens new doors, a technique that solves a problem, or an insight that simply makes sense of it all. The more you know, the smarter and faster you can go.

That's why we work with the best minds in business and finance to bring cutting-edge thinking and best learning practice to a global market.

Under a range of leading imprints, including *Financial Times Prentice Hall*, we create world-class print publications and electronic products bringing our readers knowledge, skills and understanding, which can be applied whether studying or at work.

To find out more about Pearson Education publications, or tell us about the books you'd like to find, you can visit us at
www.pearson.com/uk

Your First
100 Days

How to make maximum impact in your new leadership role

Niamh O'Keeffe

**Financial Times
Prentice Hall**
is an imprint of

Harlow, England • London • New York • Boston • San Francisco • Toronto
Sydney • Tokyo • Singapore • Hong Kong • Seoul • Taipei • New Delhi
Cape Town • Madrid • Mexico City • Amsterdam • Munich • Paris • Milan

PEARSON EDUCATION LIMITED

Edinburgh Gate
Harlow CM20 2JE
Tel: +44 (0)1279 623623
Fax: +44 (0)1279 431059
Website: www.pearson.com/uk

First published in Great Britain in 2011

Pearson Education is not responsible for the content of third-party internet sites.

ISBN: 978–0–273–75132–8

British Library Cataloguing-in-Publication Data
A catalogue record for this book is available from the British Library

Library of Congress Cataloging-in-Publication Data
O'Keeffe, Niamh.
    Your first 100 days : how to make maximum impact in your new leadership role / Niamh O'Keeffe.
        p. cm.
    Includes index.
    ISBN 978-0-273-75132-8 (pbk.)
  1. Executives. 2. Executive ability. 3. Leadership. 4. Business planning.
5. Management. I. Title. II. Title: Your first one hundred days.
    HD38.2.O42 2011
    658.4'092--dc23
                        2011026905

10 9 8 7 6 5 4 3 2 1
15 14 13 12 11

Typeset in 11/15pt Myriad Pro Regular by 3
Printed by Ashford Colour Press Ltd., Gosport

I would like to dedicate this book to all First100 clients.
Thank you.

Contents

Preface: First100™
www.First100coaching.com

SPECIALISTS IN COACHING SENIOR EXECUTIVES IN THE FIRST 100 DAYS OF A NEW LEADERSHIP APPOINTMENT

Through my experience as a headhunter placing senior executives in the City of London, I realised that the first 100 days were the most crucial stage in the lifecycle of a new leadership appointment. The first 100 days of a new role have a major determining factor on overall leadership performance and impact in the first 12 months and beyond. For example, this is the time when you have optimal licence to refresh the vision, improve the strategy, reform the team and set new goals. My observation was that failure to optimise the first 100 days was probably the biggest missed trick on leadership effectiveness and performance acceleration – a lost opportunity for the leader, resulting in losses for the inherited team and the organisation as a whole. My prior background of eight years as a strategy and management consultant for Accenture meant I was well equipped to convert this insight into a new niche 'First 100 Days' leadership offering.

empowering leaders to succeed in the first 100 days

I set up First100™ in 2004, to create outcomes where everybody wins; a win for the newly appointed leader, a win for their team, organisation and market. I created a unique methodology and approach at First100™ that enables us to empower our client business leaders to step up and overcome the challenges inherent in the first 100 days of a new leadership appointment.

First100™ team

We empower leaders to triumph in the face of adversity in the first 100 days – giving them the confidence and capability to overcome the challenges and to succeed during a heightened stress period. We have a strong vision on the role and effectiveness of quality leaders, and attempt to live out that vision as a team. We take a problem-solving approach to create fresh solutions and ideas at speed. We offer practical guidance, thoughtful insights and useful advice that is immediately implementable and always grounded in commercial realism.

First100™ clients

We have emerged as the global leading specialists on coaching senior executives in the first 100 days of a new leadership appointment. Our client track record includes working with leaders from telecommunications (e.g. BT, Telefonica O2, Vodafone, Eircom), pharmaceuticals (e.g. Boston Scientific, Teva), consultancies (e.g. Accenture, Oliver Wyman), technology (e.g. Appsense, Microsoft, McAfee, Lionbridge), financial services (e.g. Barclays, Sunlife), energy (e.g. BP), FMCG (e.g. John West) and many more.

First100™ approach

Our clients consistently offer two words, 'useful' and 'insightful', to describe the First100™ approach. First100assist™ is a new framework and methodology, designed inhouse by the founder at First100™ and refined over years of experience of working with senior leaders in their first 100 days. The approach is outcome-driven and highly structured. We take into account your whole system; you as leader, your role, your organisation and the market.

First100™ Coaching Schools

2011 saw the launch of the First100™ Coaching Schools in London and New York, offering a new and groundbreaking 'Coach the Coach' programme. With our launch into coaching schools, First100™ is making our First100assist™ framework and methodology accessible on a wider scale. This programme is for internal corporate coaches, i.e. all those who work in leadership development, human resources, learning and development, and anybody involved in on-boarding critical external leadership hires and/or ensuring internal promotees' success. The programme is also open to senior executives who wish to improve their hiring manager 'on-boarding' skills.

About the author

Niamh O'Keeffe is the founder of First100, established in 2004.

> *"First100 is a niche leadership performance acceleration concept. We serve senior executives and CEOs in the First 100 days of a new leadership appointment.*
>
> *We provide our specialist 'first 100 days' coaching expertise using a unique combination of structured planning, leadership performance acceleration insights and strong results-orientation."*

Niamh has a track record of over 18 years career experience in leadership advisory services – including strategy consulting, executive search and leadership coaching.

Niamh is a transition-expert, problem-solver, idea-generator, and trusted-advisor on leadership performance acceleration. Niamh's insights in this book are based on her many years of experience working as a leadership coach and companion on the journey of senior leaders and CEOs in the first 100 days of a critical new leadership appointment.

Niamh is also a business entrepreneur and very driven to succeed on her personal mission.

> *"My personal mission is to improve the quality of leadership in the world. I am delivering on this mission via a portfolio*

of entrepreneurial businesses, the first of which was First100 established in the UK in 2004."

CEOassist is Niamh's second entrepreneurial business. It is a niche ideation and leadership advisory service for CEOs on Legacy Projects: www.CEOassist.com.

Acknowledgements

With special thanks to John Mullins who created the opportunity for this book by putting me in touch with publisher Liz Gooster at Pearson.

With special thanks to Liz for taking this book on, guiding me through the process, and offering great suggestions throughout.

Thank you to the whole Pearson team, who turned a simple manuscript into the published book you are reading today.

I would like to acknowledge my hard-working and dedicated team at First100™, especially Eimee, Fiona, Garrett and Padraig.

Thank you to my clients who gave me the opportunity to work with them in their first 100 days.

If you would like to get in touch to share your feedback on this book, or to ask me any questions about your first 100 days, please contact me at niamh.okeeffe@First100coaching.com.

For latest news, and further insights, visit www.First100coaching. com and become a First100™ member.

Introduction

- The importance of your first 100 days
- Origins of the 'First 100 Days' concept
- Why should you read this book?
- Note to reader

1 The importance of your first 100 days

The importance of your first 100 days is the difference between success and failure in this new role – and that has consequences for your whole career.

If you have a successful first 100 days, it naturally follows that you are setting yourself up for a successful first 12 months in this role. If you have a successful first 12 months in the role, then it is likely that you will make a success of your whole role. You will want to succeed in this role for its own sake – because this is your new promotion and this is the job that you are being asked to do. But look at the bigger picture too. If you get this role right, if you succeed in this role better and faster than expected, then it naturally follows that you are more likely to get promoted sooner to an even better role, even faster, and you can continue to enjoy accelerated success in your career ambitions.

get it right from the beginning and get promoted faster

The opposite is also true. If you get off to a slow start, or a 'no-start', then imagine how much more difficult it will be to claw back lost time in an attempt to succeed later. If you fail to get it right from the beginning, then you seriously risk your chances of success in this role, which can stall or reduce your future career prospects. After all, if you cannot succeed in this role, then why offer you another promotion? Seen in the context of the bigger picture of your career, the importance of your first 100 days in a senior role appointment cannot be underestimated.

2 Origins of the 'First 100 Days' concept

Originally used to describe the speed and scope of US President Roosevelt's legendary first 100 days in office – and the measure against which, later, many other US presidents and politicians have been judged in terms of the pace at which they have mobilised their own administrations – the 'First 100 Days' concept has made its way into the business lexicon to describe the early phase of a new leadership appointment. It has become an effective method of setting out a time-bounded period for the newly appointed leader to demonstrate early actions, wins and tangible deliverables to role stakeholders.

FRANKLIN D. ROOSEVELT – A LEGENDARY FIRST 100 DAYS IN OFFICE

Franklin D. Roosevelt (FDR) had his inauguration as President of the USA on 4 March 1933. It occurred in the middle of a terrifying bank panic. Historian Arthur Schlesinger described the mood at FDR's inauguration: 'It was now a matter of seeing whether a representative democracy could conquer economic collapse. It was a matter of staving off violence – even, some thought – revolution.'

Nearly 13 million people in the USA – one in four – were jobless. Nineteen million people depended upon meagre relief payments to survive. Workers lucky enough to have jobs earned, on average, only two-thirds what they made at the start of the Depression in 1929. Many of those who had money lost it: four thousand banks collapsed in the first two months of 1933. So great was the emergency, some urged dictatorial powers, but FDR rejected the suspension of constitutional government. Instead he embarked on a plan of 'Action, and Action Now' to meet this vast crisis. The speed and scope of his actions were unprecedented.

FDR's legendary 'First 100 Days' concentrated on the first part of his strategy: immediate relief. He successfully prevented a run on the banks by immediately declaring a 'bank holiday', closing all banks indefinitely until bankers and government could regain control of the situation. From 9 March to 16 June 1933, FDR sent Congress a record number of bills, all of which passed easily. The second part of his strategy was to provide long-lasting reform to the nation's economy. The First 100 Days was important because it got the New Deal off to a strong and early start, resulting in many essential programmes taken for granted in the USA today.

Many later presidents have used the 'First 100 Days' as a measure against which to mobilise their own administrations. But none has succeeded in achieving FDR's legislative agenda. In less than four months the economy was stabilised, homes and farms were saved from foreclosure, and massive

▶

> relief and work programmes addressed the dire needs of the people. Most important, the First 100 Days restored hope and, in the process, preserved democratic government in the USA.

See any interesting parallels between FDR and the challenges that faced President Barack Obama in his first 100 days in office? Faced with considerable pressure to get the American economy and the global economy back on track, it is worth noting that one of Obama's first actions as President Elect was to announce his Two Year Plan – hitting the ground running so fast that, even though there can be only one American president at a time, he had to demonstrate a fast start months ahead of his official day one.

Your first 100 days context will not be as dramatic as that of President Roosevelt or President Obama. Nonetheless, leaders in today's high-performance corporate organisations do find themselves in extremely pressurised situations and need to be able to take charge and step up with speed, if they want to stand out from the crowd and be regarded as a strong leader.

3 Why should you read this book?

You should read this book if you are:

- *joining a new company or you are recently promoted within your own company* – if you have recently had the trigger event of being appointed as a new external hire to a senior leadership position in a new company, or new internal promotion within your existing company, congratulations and this is the right book for you. This book will provide you with the answers you seek in the form of easy-to-digest, bite-sized insights in a highly structured format;

- *ambitious* – this book is for the modern global leader – typically in their 30s and early 40s having achieved fast-track careers to date, often promoted ahead of their peers, and still very keen to continue to succeed in their career, possibly all the way to group CEO. This book will be of value to you because it examines new angles, new ideas and offers the ambitious leader an extra edge;

- *time-pressured* – when time pressures bear upon us, we want immediate gratification and instant help. You will be impatient for the answers to your problems as quickly as possible. This book gives you that instant solution within a 100-minute read. Take this book with you on your next train or plane ride, and it will make great use of your travel time, resulting in the most productive journey you have ever taken;

- *anxious not to fail* – anybody who has just received a big promotion will be determined to succeed and anxious not to fail. A big promotion is an important move and the personal stakes will feel enormous. You will be seeking some answers, some insider information – a way in – and this book offers reassurance on those answers and will give you the comfort and security of learning the best way to prepare for the role, writing your First 100 Days Plan, and executing it with success.

companies and shareholders need their leaders to perform better and faster than ever before

- *smart, senior, successful* – I noticed that a lot of business books are aimed at managers, and not the senior leaders in organisations. This book will be of value to you because it is intellectually stretching and insightful – written for smart, senior, successful leaders – and is not dumbed down or oversimplified.

The benefits of reading this book are that it will empower you to:

- hit the ground running and succeed faster;
- cope with intense time pressures;
- manage role stakeholders, when the stakes are high.

And … please realise that:

- your company 'on-boarding' solutions will not be sufficient;
- 'ability to transition' is an underestimated skill;
- your career depends on it.

In addition, the distinguishing features of this book are that it is:

- a 100-day timeline approach;
- a 100-minute speed read;
- 100 per cent practical.

HIT THE GROUND RUNNING AND SUCCEED FASTER

The book's purpose is to coach you, the reader, through the real-time challenge of the first 100 days of your new role: through a combination of structured planning, commercial insight and leadership coaching, via a 100-minute speed read. This book offers practical guidance, thoughtful insights and useful advice in bite-sized portions, which are easily understood and immediately implementable – how to write a First 100 Days Plan, backed up by a timeline and process view on what to do at each of the key milestones @ 30 days, @ 60 days, @ 90 days.

With our expert help and specialist knowledge on how to help senior executives make the most of their first 100 days, you will be able to hit the ground running faster, and achieve that extra leadership edge necessary to succeed faster on impact.

COPE WITH INTENSE TIME PRESSURES

Newly appointed leaders are compelled to have a great first 100 days because now, more than ever, the pressure is on to recover high returns on investments. Performance acceleration is a critical business demand in today's global economy. A few decades ago investors sought 10-year strategic plans, then five-year and, subsequently, three-year plans were in vogue. Since 2007 I have noticed the emergence of the 'Two-Year Plan' coming from forward-thinking CEOs and business leaders.

For chief executives of companies listed on the stock market, the first 100 days is the approximate time between the day they start a new job and Wall Street's appraisal of their performance. And, if you're not the chief executive, you are under just as much pressure from your boss and stakeholders to show a fast return on their investment in you. Directors are commanding six-figure salaries, and recruitment fees for external hires are extremely high. Executives no longer have the luxury of being in a role for 12 months before judgements are made about their worth.

time is up for the first three months to be seen as the 'settling in' period

In this ever-shrinking time-pressure context, the first 100 days of a new leadership role appointment becomes increasingly important. Time is up for the first three months to be seen as the 'settling in' period.

MANAGE ROLE STAKEHOLDERS, WHEN THE STAKES ARE HIGH

In addition to time pressures, you will be experiencing stakeholder pressure to deliver to high performance agendas. Senior appointments are not made lightly – typically the stakes are high, a significant change or turnaround is necessary and people are looking to the new leader for answers and a clear pathway forward.

The hiring manager, incumbent team and other role stakeholders in the organisation typically view a new leadership appointment with a mixture of relief and apprehension. The first phase of a new leadership appointment not only represents a fresh starting point, but also raises concerns about how to make it work. It is a time of intense mutual scrutiny, and a successful first 100 days has a major determining impact on success within the first 12 months and beyond.

YOUR COMPANY 'ON-BOARDING' SOLUTION WILL NOT BE SUFFICIENT

Through my experience as a headhunter placing senior executives in the City of London, I realised that, whilst significant time and attention were given to recruitment and assessment of potential hires, there was disproportionately little or no attention paid to their effective transition into an organisation. Although it seems so obvious to me that everybody would benefit from specialist third-party help to make the leadership step up or to acclimatise successfully into a new organisation – it seems that your organisation and human resources department have not made the same intellectual leap. While they may refer to your first 100 days as being important and there may be some 'noise' about what they will do to set you up for success, I can assure you that I have worked with the best global corporations in the world, and I have never yet come across an internal organisational solution that adequately serves the newly appointed senior external hire or senior internal promotee.

Regardless of whether an internal organisation 'on-boarding' solution exists in some guise for external hires, there is rarely any kind of process to support internal promotees to step up and succeed in a new role. This book fills the void, and offers support to internal promotees who find it even more difficult to make an impact when appointed into a new role within the same company.

'ABILITY TO TRANSITION' IS AN UNDERESTIMATED LEADERSHIP SKILL

You can be the best possible hire, but there is a skill to making a transition and an effective transition needs to occur before your talents can shine. Through my own observation I watched talented hires fail to succeed, again and again – and I observed that this resulted in wasted opportunities all round; at a minimum significant frustration, at a maximum job loss, for a talented individual, a waste of expensive recruitment fees and time invested for the organisation, and a leadership loss for the team who inevitably lacked leadership prior to the new appointee and once again has had to endure a leadership failure, another leadership gap and another attempted leadership restart with the next hire.

YOUR CAREER DEPENDS ON IT

Notwithstanding the responsibility on the leader to consider the impact on the team and organisation at large, the talented ambitious senior executive is also self-motivated to accelerate performance success in the first 100 days in order to enjoy accelerated career success.

Judgements on a fast-track leader's success in the first 100 days of a new role can be followed quickly by judgements about his or her leadership potential for success in the next step-up role in two to three years' time. It is as simple as this – if you care enough to do a good job in your first 100 days, so much so that you hire expert help via a First100™ Coach or read a First100™ book, then obviously you will do a better job than without the expertise – and therefore you will be noticed by your boss and others, and promotion naturally follows. Simple logic says that getting expert help is better and faster than going it alone. It is not unusual for a client of mine to gain further promotion within 12 months. I have worked with clients on consecutive promotions, so it's good for my business too!

100-DAY TIMELINE APPROACH

The book is organised to coach you through the real-time challenge of the first 100 days of a new role appointment. This book offers you a highly structured 100-day timeline approach; how to prepare pre-start, how to develop a First 100 Days Plan, how to tackle each key milestone @ 30 days, @ 60 days, @ 90days – and how to successfully close out at the end of 100 days.

100-MINUTE SPEED READ

In keeping with the underlying theme of accelerated performance, this book is organised in a 'speed read' style for the time-pressured leader. Time is often considered a scarce resource but never more so than at the beginning of a new role appointment when the pressure is on to deliver results, and quickly. Deliberately concise, this book provides the crucial insights in 100 minutes to empower you, the time-pressured leader, to achieve the greatest success during this intense early phase.

this book gives you the crucial insights in 100 minutes

100 PER CENT PRACTICAL

This book is a coach and companion to help you to perform better and faster, by setting out the right set of 100-day desired outcomes, and showing you how to achieve them. The first 100 days is a pressurised moment of need, and intellectualisation of the issues won't help. This book offers you a structured approach, practical guidance, thoughtful insights and useful advice – all easily understood and immediately implementable.

4 Note to reader

Dear Reader,

You are an important person, because you are a leader with responsibility for others. I see you as a whole person: an emotional being as well as a business brain and a talented being. I see you as a learner, open to guidance and advice because you are stepping up to a role that you have never done before.

it is make or break time

In the first 100 days, even more so than at any other time in the lifecycle of a leadership appointment, all eyes are on you. It is a time of pressure, of intense scrutiny. It is make or break time as to whether you lay down the right foundation for the rest of your first year and beyond.

I want to help you achieve success in your first 100 days, so that everybody benefits: you, your team, the organisation who hired or promoted you, and all your role stakeholders.

I have stepped back from my day-to-day role, as First100™ Coach, and attempted to gather my specialist First 100 Days knowledge and experience into a book that is useful to you.

Please enjoy reading this book. I hope you find it both strategic and pragmatic in its approach, with some good ideas and insights, grounded in the commercial reality of your situation.

Wishing you well on your First 100 Days journey.

Niamh O'Keeffe

part one

Beginning

The nature of beginnings: role beginnings bring a heady mix of excitement, anticipation and nervousness too. There is a feeling of being the 'special one' – singled out from others to take on an important role. However, there is also a feeling of trepidation – am I really good enough? Will I succeed or fail?

will I succeed or fail?

Leaders, however experienced, are emotional beings just like everybody else. In my experience, everybody who is facing their first 100 days oscillates between these feelings of 'special one/superiority' and 'worried one/inferiority'. Regulating your emotions during the beginning stage of your first 100 days is an important key to your success. At the beginning of an important role appointment, some executives feel overwhelmed by a feeling of panic and fear of failure. Others are over-confident and completely underestimate the challenges ahead. Try to stay centred from the beginning. If you can stay grounded, and can feel calm and confident in yourself from the beginning, you are giving yourself a chance to make the best possible start in the role.

It might seem like an odd thing, especially to junior people who think their leaders always know what to do, but I have noticed that, very often, senior executives simply don't know how to get started properly in a new role. After all, there is so much to do – sometimes it can be very difficult to know how to take that first step and start. The temptation is to simply dive in and tackle the first problem that presents itself, and then the next and the next. This approach of getting stuck in is their answer on how to start. It's one way, but it is not the best way – it is too short-termist, too reactive and it is certainly not the most thoughtful or strategic way to tackle a new role appointment!

In the forthcoming chapters, I outline an approach and key steps for what you can do to prepare before you officially start in the role, and what you should do when you start.

Prepare

1 Let go of your previous role.

2 Set up your energy management system.

3 Understand the key transition challenges.

4 Build profile of role, organisation, market.

5 Start with the end in mind.

@ start

1 Launch your First 100 Days Plan.

2 Show up as a leader, not a manager.

3 Bring 'sizzle' as well as substance.

4 EQ will be as important as IQ.

5 Critical success factors for the next 30 days: day 1–30

First100™ client case study

JOHN, NEWLY APPOINTED GLOBAL HEAD OF SALES FOR PREMIUM SERVICES, ABC BANK

'It's great I got the job, but now what?!'
At 39 years old, and a relatively young member of his company's European leadership team, John was surprised but pleased to get the call from the group CEO and learn of his unexpectedly fast promotion into a global leadership

▶

role as global head of sales for Premium Services at the Bank. He would be responsible for sales and marketing of the premium services business banking division, initially focusing the client strategy across Europe and Asia.

The existing role holder, Brian, had unexpectedly resigned to join the competition. Due to the confidential nature of the role, and his defection to the competition, Brian had been accompanied out of the building by security – so a seamless handover was certainly out of the question! John did not know what team issues he would inherit from his predecessor – but he remembered hearing that Brian used an old-fashioned style of management, was very hierarchical and tended to create divisions in his team by relying on a few favourites in his inner circle to get things done.

The Asian market would be extremely important. However, none of the Asian stakeholders internally or externally are familiar with John. Relationship management in Asia is crucial and this meant John was already on the back foot in terms of getting things done via relationship goodwill alone.

The company was facing significant shareholder pressure to deliver high growth returns quickly, and John's revenue and growth potential represented up to 10 per cent of global company revenues. The team he would inherit was a mixed group in terms of capability, and he already knew from conversations with the CEO that his first job would be to fire someone on the team who had recently been found lacking on fulfilling the ethical company standards expected in his role.

The team were upset by the sudden departure of Brian,

and were unsure as to what kind of working style they could expect from their new boss. After all, he was younger than most of them. Some members of the team resented the company's recent policy on fast-tracking younger talent who may be bright but who, in their view, lacked the necessary years of experience.

Putting the required firing aside, it was not immediately obvious to John what to do or how to start to tackle the whole role. This was not a well-established position, it was created only four years ago in response mainly to the Asia opportunity and there was no actual job description. His boss was the group CEO – with many pressing priorities of his own – and simply expected John to get on with it and define his own role and leadership goals. This was one of those 'sink or swim' high-intensity roles – high reward, but high risk from a career perspective too.

John's current role responsibilities and existing issues tied him in until the calendar year end, and until he appointed a successor – so that meant the next eight weeks would be about how to close out the current job and finding a successor, with surely no time to even think about the new job.

John was ambitious and he knew that, if he did well in this role, it would bode well for fast-track promotion to the group executive committee.

Suddenly the pressure of the promotion felt enormous. At 4 am on Monday morning, with two weeks to go until start date, John tossed and turned, unable to sleep. *'It's great I got the job, but now what?!'*

1

Prepare

- Let go of your previous role
- Set up your energy management system
- Understand the key transition challenges
- Build profile of role, organisation and market
- Start with the end in mind

1 Let go of your previous role

Saying your first step is to hand over your current role may seem like stating the obvious but, in my experience, people do not detach fast enough.

Letting go of current attachments as quickly as possible is a crucial first step because you need to refocus all your time, energy and thoughts on the new role. So, remember, however committed a person you are – your last role was your responsibility, but it is not your responsibility any more. As soon as you hand in your notice, start to close out the previous role immediately.

it is over, so hand it over

Some senior executives stay involved in their previous role for all the wrong reasons:

- preference to stay in comfort zone;
- concern about managing their legacy;
- emotional ties to team;
- false belief that no one else could be good enough to take over.

I always check that my clients are 100 per cent detached from their old role, and 100 per cent focused on the new role – otherwise, we are off to a slow start!

If you're an internal appointee (like John in our Case Study example) then letting go can be understandably harder than for an external hire that contractually leaves his or her company and physically leaves a building.

Your internal transition may also be tougher if you are expected to do both roles until your successor is found. Add to this the fact that, as an internal appointee, you are already a known entity, 'institutionalised' and most likely pre-programmed on the issues. It's tough to bring a fresh perspective if you have always been there. Let's face it, an external appointee with none of the internal baggage may have an initial advantage simply by turning up.

Accelerating success in your first 100 days is already compromised if you are attempting to overlap two jobs at once, so what can an internal appointee do to get off to an accelerated start in the first 100 days?

Internal promotees need to be very assertive and artificially re-create the same context of an external hire:

- negotiate a clear finishing date for current role;
- appoint an interim if your successor is not in situ and fully hand over;
- agree a formal starting date of new role, and don't start until then.

2 Set up your energy management system

The first 100 days is an intense phase – all eyes are on you and there is considerable pressure to perform and deliver early. So, in preparation, create time in between roles to rest, recover from your previous role and get ready for the new challenge ahead.

Think of yourself as a corporate athlete resting between serious races.

you need to be fit for purpose, with a surplus of energy

My suggestion to clients is to take a minimum of two weeks' full-time holiday break in between roles. This will clear your head from the old role and heighten energy levels and perspective coming into the first 100 days of the new role. You need to be fit for purpose, with a surplus of energy to take on a new role and make a strong early impact.

Table 1.1 Energy management in your first 100 days

Take care of your mind	Before, during and after work, schedule enough time and space to be on your own so that you can relax and release the build-up of pressure.
Take care of your body	Exercise routinely, eat healthy and nutritious food. Try to build up extra reserve in your system.
Enlist others to support you	Get third-party help. Find an internal mentor. Hire an external coach. Negotiate extra support and latitude from loved ones. Maintain a calm and nurturing personal life.

Don't think that this next 100 days is business as usual in your personal life. Starting a new role is a heightened stress event. Adrenalin will compensate for any lack of reserves, but don't exacerbate the pressure on you by having the house redecorated or the in-laws coming for a visit!

Keep a cool, clear head and maintain a calm personal life if you want to enjoy accelerated success in the first 100 days.

Earlier in my coaching career I noticed a pattern of leaders feeling poorly during their first 100 days. It typically presents itself as my clients telling me, in passing, that they have a 'major cold'. And it is always accompanied with an air of surprise: 'I'm never usually ill.'

It was being mentioned as if it was a completely separate event, and not linked to the context of the heightened stress from taking up a new job – demonstrating a total lack of awareness of the cause (major stress) and effect (major cold).

Now I proactively educate my clients to acknowledge that what is going on in their bodies can represent a physical manifestation or fallout from the challenge of the first 100 days. We get ahead of the curve, by adopting tactics to manage or mitigate rising stress levels early. Having a First 100 Days Plan helps clients to feel more confident and in control and less stressed. But also I encourage my clients to make time for mind-calming exercise, such as golf or yoga. I also suggest my client carves out some regular quiet time on their own during the working day to calm the mind and reset their priorities. This can be as little as 20 minutes' quiet time in the morning and 20 minutes' quiet time in the afternoon – and yet the benefits are amazing in terms of the effect of keeping you calm and centred on the right priorities for the whole day.

First100™ client case study continued

JOHN, NEWLY APPOINTED GLOBAL HEAD OF SALES FOR PREMIUM SERVICES, ABC BANK

'It's okay to admit that you are feeling under pressure'
Although he had never previously considered getting third-party help, John was very relieved when a colleague recommended a First100™ expert he could talk to about his new role challenges. John was surprised at the experience and candour of the First100™ Coach. As John read the session notes, he realised that he had a lot to learn if he wanted to make a successful leadership step up.

▶

Coach notes from Session 1

As a coach, there is nothing more worrying than meeting a client who is under pressure prior to starting a new job, trying to convince himself and others that he is not under pressure. It raises red flags – makes me wonder if the person has any coping techniques other than trying to pretend that nothing is wrong. Admitting you're under pressure is a good thing for you and any senior executive to do, otherwise you are blocking out reality and not developing strategies to deal with a very intense job.

Every leader needs to have a suite of coping techniques to alleviate pressure because a leader's job always involves pressure – techniques can range from yoga to golf, to quiet time by oneself, walking the dog, practising meditation or scheduling regular 20-minute 'time-out' breaks during the working day.

Denial as a coping method is the kind of macho behaviour that leads men into 'sudden' heart attacks. So let's get more real; it is okay to say you're under pressure. Put it another way – how could you not be?! You're the newly appointed global head of sales for Premium Services at your bank, but your predecessor has left without a proper handover, you are massively under-resourced from a people perspective, you need to quickly build crucial relationships with important Asian stakeholders, you are concerned about hitting the quarterly numbers, you have the stress of moving offices, you're probably still jet-lagged from recent trips abroad and you said you're finding it difficult to sleep.

So, admit it, accept it, say it out loud … 'I feel under pressure. I feel overwhelmed. It's a whirlwind and it can feel out of control.'

Doing anything else makes you seem ungrounded, unrealistic, unable to face the truth.

However, if you accept it, then you have to do something about it. If you accept that you are under pressure, then you will have to start using techniques to alleviate the pressure. If you start using techniques to alleviate the pressure, you will start to alleviate and release the pressure – and like night follows day, you will feel better and start to perform better.

John had felt overwhelmed by his new responsibilities on his way into the coaching session, but had to acknowledge that he felt much calmer on the way out. Accepting that he felt under more pressure than usual was an unexpected relief in itself. It was time to stop that feeling of overwhelm from returning and getting in the way of his performance. The coach had given John ideas on how to adequately prepare for the role and, feeling better equipped on where to start, John sat at his desk and started to apply the information to his new role situation.

3 Understand the key transition challenges

The primary task for the executive targeting first 100 days success is to set out the right strategic priorities and stay focused on them.

Sounds simple? Unfortunately, it is easier said than done. There is a list of common challenges inherent in every transition that will affect the newly appointed executive. These can derail good intentions and get in the way of successfully achieving that primary task.

Key transition challenges:

- time pressures and intense learning curve;
- being overwhelmed with immediate 'fire-fighting' and task-driven priorities;
- need to invest energy in building new networks and forging new stakeholder relationships;
- dealing with legacy issues from the predecessor;
- challenges on inheriting or building a team and having to make tough personnel decisions;
- for external hires, a lack of experience of new company culture may lead to inadvertent gaffes and early political blunders – all of which can take time to recover;
- getting the balance right between moving too fast and moving too slowly.

Each one is worthy of consideration, so read through the list and take some time to reflect on how each of these transition challenges applies to your context.

Go through the list of key transition challenges in Table 1.2, and apply each one to your own unique circumstances to gain a greater appreciation of what lies ahead for you.

Table 1.2 Key transition challenges

Time pressures and intense learning curve	It takes time to get up to speed on the content of your new position, and yet business and markets cannot slow down and wait for you to catch up. Decisions still need to be taken and, consequently, the pressure can build up and will need to be managed in order to stay operating effectively.
Being overwhelmed with immediate 'fire-fighting' and task-driven priorities	It would be tempting to 'get busy' and dive into the immediate business tasks and issues. But you need to have the strength of character to step back, and take time out to look at the big picture: what tasks should you continue, what should you stop, and what should you start?
Need to invest energy in building new networks and forging new stakeholder relationships	There is no point in having the right vision and strategy in isolation of bringing people with you. The culture may be dense and slow moving – people may be resistant to the changes you bring. Invest early in the influencer and stakeholder network.
Dealing with legacy issues from the predecessor	Depending on the quality of your predecessor, your unit may or may not have a good reputation, and your team may have developed poor habits, behaviours and disciplines that will take time to address. Or you may have to endure the scenario of filling the shoes of a much-loved predecessor and being resented as the new guy whose mandate is to change how things have always been done before.
Challenges on inheriting or building a team and having to make tough personnel decisions	Don't expect underperformers to have been weeded out prior to your arrival. A key task in your first 100 days will be to assess the quality of your team: who stays, who goes and who else is needed onboard. And, unfortunately, your best performer is probably now de-motivated and resentful – and consequently underperforming – because he applied unsuccessfully for your job.

▶

For external hires, a lack of experience of new company culture may lead to inadvertent gaffes and early political blunders – all of which can take time to recover	From the innocuous to the significant, everything you do is being judged as indicative of your character. Merely checking your BlackBerry® during a meeting may deeply offend your new role stakeholders who may judge that action as an indication that you are brash, disinterested and arrogant. You will need to be on 'hyper alert' to consciously pick up clues on the acceptable norms and behaviours.
Getting the balance right between moving too fast and moving too slowly	New appointees sometimes panic and this can result in either doing too much (scatter-gun approach, but not tackling the core issues) or doing too little ('I'll just listen for the first three months, and then decide what to do'). Neither extreme cuts it. Find the right balance.

Patient preparation and adequate awareness of what you are facing is the first step. At the 'Prepare' stage, if you can take the time out to begin to understand all the transition challenges that you face, then the sooner you can start to equip yourself with observations, insights and ideas on how to overcome or deal with them. Understanding your transition challenges is an exercise that starts to form the backdrop for developing your First 100 Days Plan.

Once you understand the transition challenges, are you then ready to write your First 100 Days Plan?

Absolutely not! In my experience, business executives are so eager to write their First 100 Days Plan that, as soon as they have a grasp on some of their challenges, they immediately want to write a list of what they need to do. However, this approach is too short-sighted, and the executive list is usually not all-encompassing because it is written too quickly and without enough thought and foresight.

Apply my 'Ready-steady-steady-go' formula for the best possible preparation before you start to write your First 100 Days Plan:

ready, steady, steady and ... go!

- Ready – first, understand your transition challenges.
- Steady – next, build a profile of your role, organisation and market.
- Steady – then, start with the strategic end in mind about what you ultimately want to achieve.
- Go – only now should you go ahead and write your First 100 Days Plan.

Have the patience to apply the 'Ready-steady-steady-go' formula!

So, right now, resist any temptation to write your First 100 Days Plan, and continue your due diligence by completing the next step: building a profile of your role, organisation and market.

4 Build profile of role, organisation and market

In addition to understanding your transition challenges, step back and take a wide-lens view of the 'whole system' within which you will be operating. See it is as a construct where you are at the centre: person (you, as leader), in a role, in an organisation, and set in the context of your marketplace (see Figure 1.1).

Build up a profile of each component in this system, in order to map out the landscape of your opportunities and challenges. Remember to take advantage of this 'Prepare' phase. After all, this is the most clear-headed you will be because soon you will

Figure 1.1 'Whole system' approach

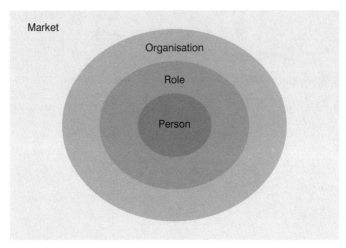

be mired in the detail and day-to-day requirements of the role. Now is the time to understand the big picture. Survey the 'whole system' landscape with as much perspective as possible, and continue to draw out information and insights on what lies ahead of you.

Profiling exercise

Profile the person (you, as leader)	● What is the leadership 'step up' for you (e.g. promotion to managing a function for the first time? A switch from functional expert to general manager? From managing a business to managing an enterprise?) .... ● What strengths, tools and experiences can you uniquely bring to the role that you can leverage to make an early impact, and can accelerate early performance? ....
Profile the role	● Is there a learning curve on industry, product, strategy that you can start to tackle now, ahead of starting? ....

- What have you been asked to do? What are the expected role deliverables?

....
....
....
....
....
....

- What do you know about the capability of your team? What are the gaps?

....
....
....
....
....
....

- Find out what has been communicated to others about you and your mandate.

....
....
....
....
....
....

Profile the organisation	- What is your vision for the role? How does your vision for this role link to the vision and mission of the organisation? How can you create value for the organisation? ....

- Look at the company website to profile the CEO and top leadership team. Who are your role stakeholders? Who are the key decision makers, who are the influencers, who are the potential blockers?

....
....
....
....
....
....

- What do you know about the culture of this organisation, unit, team – its norms and values? Who can you meet prior to starting that can give you more information on the ways of working at this company?

....
....
....
....
....
....

Profile the market/world system	- Consider the market – who is your customer (internal and/or external)? Who are your competitors? What is the biggest market challenge facing you in this role? What are the market dynamics, e.g. growth versus decline?

....
....
....
....
....
....

Using the clues in the preceding profiling exercise, take time to think widely and deeply to build up the picture of what you are facing, so that you understand more quickly and navigate the whole system in the first 100 days.

At this 'Prepare' phase, don't rush to judgement too early. You may have some information at this stage but, remember, you have not met all the players yet, and you don't have experience of the actual role yet. Be like a detective who has clues, but not yet all of the information pieced together. Find the right balance of building up a profile of what is ahead and, at the same time, reserve final judgement so that you can wisely allow reality and your own personal experience to adjust your perspective once you have started.

5 Start with the end in mind

There is one final preparation step to complete before you are ready to write your First 100 Days Plan. To date, you have focused effort on understanding your transition challenges and building up a picture of the role, the organisation and the market. This has been very important as a way of gathering information about the past and current context. But what about the future? What is it that you want to achieve with this role? If you were to fast-forward to two years from now, how would you like to describe your successes and the new state of play?

If you think more strategically about the future and your vision for this role, then it means you will be more strategic about what you have to achieve in your first 100 days. By starting with the strategic end in mind, you are more likely to come up with new strategic initiatives to be completed in your first 100 days.

Start with the end in mind:

1 Envisage a two-year role horizon
   - what do you want to have achieved within two years in this role?
2 Establish your first 12-month strategic priorities
   - given what you want to achieve within two years, what are your priorities in the first 12 months?

… and only then are you ready to put all the pieces together and write your First 100 Days Plan.

Gathering information for this exercise may require you to meet your boss and key role stakeholders before officially starting in your new role, but usually this will be welcomed and accommodated – and will be seen as a positive mark of your enthusiasm for the role. Try not to overwhelm them with too much 'newbie' enthusiasm before you start(!) but it should be okay to set up a relatively informal pre-joining coffee/introductions meeting, and you can use the time to gather the information you need.

if you don't know where you are going, you will end up in the wrong place

1 ENVISAGE A TWO-YEAR ROLE HORIZON

Write a list of what you would like to have achieved with this role by the end of the two years on:

● vision and strategy;
● people and teams;
● results and deliverables.

TWO-YEAR ROLE ASPIRATIONS	MY LIST OF DESIRED OUTCOMES TO BE ACHIEVED BY THE END OF TWO YEARS
On vision and strategy	.... Example: 'We are the "go to" provider of Premium Services in our industry. We outrank the competition on product mix, value-for-money, customer service, and employer of choice.'
On people and teams	.... Examples: ● A dynamic leadership team in place ● A positive work culture ● People want to work here ● Our teams feel connected globally
On results and deliverables	.... Examples: ● £ sales and % growth targets achieved ● We have a reputation for getting things done ● Proven results track record across all our metrics ● Robust financials including healthy sales pipeline

Even if your role contract is for three years or more or timelines unstated, my advice is that you assume you are leaving in two years. This gives you a sense of urgency in which to 'attack' the core role challenges. And if you take a view that you can do a three-year role in two years, then you are more likely to be promoted into your next role faster! With timelines shrinking even faster than ever before, it's more realistic for high-performing leaders to assume a two-year role tenure and, either way, it forces the pace. Seeing three years into the future is harder than ever. Two years is just about possible. And anything less than two years results in too much unhelpful short-termism, reactive tactics and is not a conducive mindset for vision development and strategic planning. If your role tenure lasts beyond two years, you can simply reset your plans, as you enter into a new two-year rhythm.

Please note that there is a problematic downside at times in the case of leaders who operate with a two-year role horizon – if they accelerate pace but compromise long-term strategy and investments. My advice to executives is to remember that their role legacy will come back to haunt their long-term career if they don't get it right, so don't focus on short-term gains only, think about your role contribution in a stewardship fashion and how your lasting legacy and reputation in each role lives beyond the lifetime of your appointment.

2 ESTABLISH YOUR FIRST 12-MONTH STRATEGIC PRIORITIES

Having set out your list of desired outcomes to be achieved within two years, now write your list of first 12-month strategic priorities in that context, also taking the time to sense-check your list against everything you have already learned regarding:

● key transition challenges;

- your profiling of the role, organisation and market;
- early stakeholder conversations.

When you consider the early stakeholder conversations or the role requirements outlined during the recruitment interviews or promotion process, take into account that this recruitment phase may have included a 'selling' of the role to you – and some difficult challenges or priorities may have been mentioned but, perhaps, not in all their full glorious detail! It happens more frequently than it should that, for external recruits, the selling process may even have involved taking out or 'softening' the true reality of the challenges of the role. Also, if you had to give three or more months' notice before starting, it is inevitable that priorities will have shifted and new external factors are in the mix by now. So, what you may need to do before you can write your First 100 Days Plan is to sit down with your boss to reconfirm and agree in detail the 12-month business priorities.

Clearly, this is also the opportunity to solicit information from your boss on what is expected from you in the first 100 days. Take this as input for your First 100 Days Plan, because, of course, ideally you would want to do more than what is expected.

Your strategic aspirations

TWO-YEAR ROLE ASPIRATIONS	MY LIST OF DESIRED OUTCOMES TO BE ACHIEVED BY THE END OF TWO YEARS	FIRST 12-MONTH STRATEGIC PRIORITIES
On vision and strategy	.... Example: 'We are the "go to" provider of Premium Services in our industry. We outrank the competition on product mix, value-for-money, customer service, and employer of choice.'	.... Example: Clear business strategy in operation, with clients back at the heart of our product proposition.
On people and teams	.... Examples: ● A dynamic leadership team in place ● A positive work culture ● People want to work here ● Our teams feel connected globally	.... Examples: ● End of year employee survey ranks us as number one division in the company to work for ● New director of customer experience appointed ● Fresh talent identified and brought onto the team

▶

TWO-YEAR ROLE ASPIRATIONS	MY LIST OF DESIRED OUTCOMES TO BE ACHIEVED BY THE END OF TWO YEARS	FIRST 12-MONTH STRATEGIC PRIORITIES
On results and deliverables	....	....
	Examples: ● *£ sales and % growth targets achieved* ● *We have a reputation for getting things done* ● *Proven results track record across all our metrics* ● *Robust financials including healthy sales pipeline*	Examples: ● *Quarterly sales and growth targets achieved* ● *On track to exceed £m annual target sales revenue* ● *Healthy sales pipeline in place*

JOHN, NEWLY APPOINTED GLOBAL HEAD OF SALES FOR PREMIUM SERVICES, ABC BANK

'Get ready to write your First 100 Days Plan'

John sat with his coach to discuss his role preparations to date. Never before had he prepared so thoroughly for a new role, and John now felt much more confident about the road ahead.

John explained to his coach that an examination of his transition challenges made him realise that he needed to invest more time early on bonding with his team, and the wider group of people in his division, to ensure that they felt connected to him as their new leader, and more motivated to perform. John could see three types of groups he needed to pay attention to during his first 100 days; his direct report team (directors), their teams (senior managers), and finally all others (manager level and below). Depending on the category, John could arrange different meeting and communications formats – from one-to-ones with his direct reports to group meetings with senior managers, and a town-hall/social event with all others. John knew it was the right thing to do to set aside time early on for mutual listening and mutual understanding. He realised he had been in danger of focusing all his time and efforts touring Asia and building his new client relationships and he admitted to his coach that, if he hadn't stopped to prepare adequately, he might have neglected to touch base with his teams in the first 100 days.

▶

John had the opportunity of meeting some of his senior team members as part of his preparations, and he was surprised at their slow pace of decision making. Everybody was waiting for him to turn up and take charge, and tell them what to do. It seemed like this team were very used to their leader telling them what to do, every step of the way. John explained to his coach that his leadership style would be completely different from that of his predecessor. John didn't want team members to wait to be told what to do. John's style was to set out clear expectations of goals to be achieved, but he preferred his team members to use their own initiative on the how. By reflecting on his predecessor's leadership style and preference for people to be dependent on being told what to do, John realised that he would need to invest time in his first 100 days 'retraining' and empowering his direct reports. In discussion with his coach, John realised that this point of difference might be a very positive change and might inspire much better performance from his team, but it was about communicating this message in the right way.

As John spoke, his coach encouraged him to take notes of these key insights, as they would all need to be reflected in his First 100 Days Plan. 'What about the profiling exercise?' asked his coach. 'Was this a worthwhile use of your time?'

John replied that he now had a more thorough understanding of the big picture. Firstly he had reflected on the nature of his own leadership step up, and how he needed to change from being a functional expert in sales to more of a general manager of people. John had also invested time in profiling the market, and realised that the market was getting more competitive as new players had recently entered and were jostling for position. When he applied the technique of 'starting with the end in mind' John realised his division had to become more strategic about what products they offered. By thinking more clearly about what he wanted to achieve with the role within two years, he realised that the team needed to take a completely fresh look at how they were going to market. As John and his coach talked it through, John had a new idea about dividing the team into 'strategic cells' of three and having each cell focused on key strategic leapfrog moves.

John felt even more energised about the task ahead. He listened attentively as his coach explained how to take all these insights and organise them in a way that culminated in writing an optimal First 100 Days Plan.

Your First 100 Days Plan

● First100assist™ framework

Now you are ready to write your First 100 Days Plan.

You need to bear in mind all the information you have gathered to date, in terms of:

● transition challenges;
● profile of role, organisation and market;
● two-year role vision, and 12-month strategic priorities.

With all that information as context, your First 100 Days Plan should set out what you want to have achieved by the end of the first 100 days. Your plan should be structured using monthly milestones (@ 30 days, @ 60 days, @ 90 days) to facilitate monthly reviews and keep your plan on track.

In my experience, executives usually don't write proper First 100 Day Plans. Instead they write lists. They have either a set of themes or a list of things to do in their first 100 days, and they confuse this with having a plan.

Also, surprisingly, executives tend to narrow their role rather than see it in its full expansive glory. For example, executives tend to view their role as their individual functional area, rather than remember that they must also be a team member at peer level and deliver value in the wider sphere of being a leader of the firm. Faced with the enormity of a new role, and new context, many executives oversimplify their plan by focusing on one key deliverable, e.g. the new marketing director focuses on delivering the marketing plan. And then, subsequently, they focus on the next task, e.g. building the team. This linear single-tasking approach makes for a very slow start.

a set of key themes or a to-do list is not a First 100 Days plan

If you truly want to accelerate your performance and deliver massive early success in a manageable way, then read on and I will explain the First100™ approach to crafting an optimal First 100 Days Plan.

First100assist™ framework

Since 2004, we have developed hundreds of First 100 Day Plans. We have continuously improved our approach in response to our clients' needs. As such, we have amassed considerable experience and expertise on what constitutes a best practice First 100 Days Plan. With that as context, I designed the First100assist™ framework whereby, for the purposes of First 100 Days, we take any leadership role and reframe it by splitting it across a whole system view and devising 10 key constituent roles.

In the first 100 days of your leadership role, we believe you have to be:

- **on person:** *transition maker, unique contributor;*
- **on role:** *content learner, business achiever, team builder, communications provider;*
- **on organisation:** *relationship builder, value adder, culture navigator;*
- **on market:** *market player.*

These 10 constituent roles are shown in the First100assist™ framework in Figure 2.1.

STEP 1: START WITH THE END IN MIND

What do you want to have achieved by the end of your first 100 days?

For each of the 10 constituent roles, across your 'whole system', decide what you want to have achieved by the end of the first 100 days, and then fill in the First100assist™ template with your 10 desired outcomes.

Figure 2.1 First100assist™ framework: a 'Whole system' approach

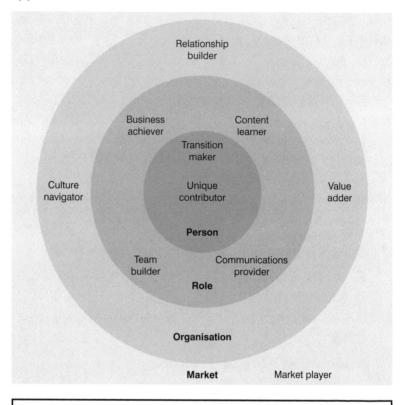

Example of John, the newly appointed global head of sales for Premium Services, ABC Bank

The person (you, as leader)

1 Transition maker – what is your leadership skills step up?
Desired outcome: by the end of the first 100 days, my desired outcome on transition maker is to have achieved the following

....
....
....

For example:
– Made an effective leadership skills transition from managing 500 people in Europe to leading a team of 3,000 across Europe and Asia.

2 Unique contributor – what unique attributes or strengths can you capitalise on for the benefit of everybody?

Desired outcome: by the end of the first 100 days, my desired outcome on unique contributor is to have achieved the following

....

....

....

For example:

– Capitalised on my communications strength to reach out and inspire my entire group of 3,000 people. Re-energised the 'premium services' division and helped people to feel more engaged and connected to the company vision and the role we play in successfully achieving it.

The role

3 Content learner – what is your learning curve/content knowledge gap?

Desired outcome: by the end of the first 100 days, my desired outcome on content learner is to have achieved the following

....

....

....

For example:

– Gained an expert understanding of our customer needs, what our existing 'premium services' product set delivers, and opportunities diagnosed for strategic innovation.

4 Business achiever – what are your key role deliverables?

Desired outcome: by the end of the first 100 days, my desired outcome on business achiever is to have achieved the following

....

....

....

For example:

– Delivered high impact £££ quick win on Premium Services strategy
– Improved Premium Services processes and team
– Fresh insights into key customers in Asia: completed new customer segmentation analysis.

(Note: I would expect a bulleted list under the desired outcome for 'business achiever' because these are probably the most obvious tasks and tangible deliverables associated with your role contribution.)

▶

5 Team builder – what can you do to build a high-performing team?

Desired outcome: by the end of the first 100 days, my desired outcome on team builder is to have achieved the following

....

....

....

For example:

– Restructured the team, replaced the marketing director, recruited fresh talent, reassigned roles and responsibilities aligned with our two-year vision.

6 Communications provider – what communications architecture will work for you in this company?

Desired outcome: by the end of the first 100 days, my desired outcome on communications provider is to have achieved the following

....

....

....

For example:

– Using a combination of new intranet site, twitter, blog, one-to-ones, team meetings, town halls, I will have secured buy in for my two-year vision, my 12-month priorities, my First 100 Days Plan and our progress against those priorities.

The organisation

7 Value adder – what is your vision for the role, and how can this create extra value for the company?

Desired outcome: by the end of the first 100 days, my desired outcome on value adder is to have achieved the following

....

....

....

For example:

– Refreshed the two-year vision for Premium Services Division and set out clear direction on the next 12-month priorities.

8 Relationship builder – who really matters here? Who are your role stakeholders?

Desired outcome: by the end of the first 100 days, my desired outcome on relationship builder is to have achieved the following

....

....

....

For example:

– Met my top 10 Europe and Asia stakeholders and forged strong early trusted advisor relationships.

9 Culture navigator – what do you need to do to successfully navigate this culture?

Desired outcome: by the end of the first 100 days, my desired outcome on culture navigator is to have achieved the following

....

....

....

For example:

– Improved my understanding of this new environment: how power and politics operate, how decisions are made here.

The market

10 Market player – what can you achieve in terms of a market quick-win or major impact?

Desired outcome: by the end of the first 100 days, my desired outcome on market player is to have achieved the following

....

....

....

For example:

– Announced a new market insight and a fast proposition into the Premium Services marketplace.

Take your 10 desired outcomes and write them as a bullet point list on one page. These should now represent your 10 most important high-level priorities in the first 100 days.

Stop and check, is there anything you have inadvertently missed in your top 10 list? Go back over your transition challenges, the profiling exercise, and what you wanted to achieve within a two-year role horizon. Is every key point adequately reflected at a high level under one of these top 10 desired outcomes?

Example of John, the newly appointed global head of sales for Premium Services, ABC Bank

FIRST 100 DAYS PLAN: TOP 10 DESIRED OUTCOMES TO BE ACHIEVED BY THE END OF MY FIRST 100 DAYS

Transition maker	Made an effective leadership skills transition from managing 500 people in Europe to leading a team of 3,000 across Europe and Asia
Unique contributor	Capitalised on my communications strength to reach out and inspire my entire group of 3,000 people. Re-energised the 'Premium Services' division and helped people to feel more engaged and connected to the company vision and the role we play in successfully achieving it
Content learner	Gained an expert understanding of our customer needs, what our existing 'Premium Services' product set delivers, and opportunities diagnosed for strategic innovation
Business achiever	<ul><li>Delivered high impact £££ quick win on Premium Services strategy</li><li>Improved Premium Services processes and team</li><li>Gained greater insight into key customers in Asia: completed new customer segmentation analysis</li></ul>

Team builder	Restructured the team, replaced the marketing director, recruited fresh talent, reassigned roles and responsibilities aligned with our two-year vision
Communications provider	Using a combination of new intranet site, Twitter, blog, one-to-ones, team meetings, town halls, I will have secured buy-in for my two-year vision, my 12-month priorities, my First 100 Days Plan and our progress against those priorities
Value adder	Refreshed the two-year vision for Premium Services Division and set out clear direction on next 12-month priorities
Relationship builder	Met my top 10 Europe and Asia stakeholders and forged strong early trusted advisor relationships
Culture navigator	Improved my understanding of this environment: how power and politics operate, how decisions are made here
Market player	Announced a new market insight and a fast proposition into the Premium Services marketplace

STEP 2: BREAK DOWN DESIRED OUTCOMES INTO @ 30, @ 60 AND @ 90 MILESTONES

Having set out your list of 10 most important desired outcomes, the next step is to break down each desired outcome into monthly milestones of 30 days/60 days/90 days preceded by initial first-step actions. You can see how this works in the following slide example – write your desired outcome at the top of the slide and break it down into manageable timeline tasks underneath;

immediate first steps, what you want to achieve by the end of 30 days, what you want to achieve by the end of 60 days and, finally, what you want to achieve by the end of 90 days.

Example of template slide

First 100 Days Plan

Desired outcome: ....

FIRST STEPS	BY THE END OF 30 DAYS	BY THE END OF 60 DAYS	BY THE END OF 90 DAYS

So, for each desired outcome, list the first steps to be taken and list the interim outcomes to be achieved by each 30-day milestone. You will end up with 10 slides in total – one for each of the 10 desired outcomes.

First step actions

This is the list of first-step activities/actions you need to take.

- Taking each desired outcome, one at a time, what do you need to do as one or more immediate first steps?

Monthly milestone outcomes

This is not a list of all the day-to-day activities or actions you need to take. These are the monthly outcomes you want to have achieved by each milestone to know you are on track to achieving your desired outcome by the end of 100 days.

By the end of 30 days

- What would you need to have achieved by the end of 30 days, to know you are on track to achieving your desired outcome by the end of 100 days? (Fill in the 'by the end of 30 days' box.)

By the end of 60 days:

- What would you need to have achieved by the end of 60 days, to know you are on track to achieving your desired outcome by the end of 100 days? (Fill in the 'by the end of 60 days' box.)

By the end of 90 days

- What would you need to have achieved by the end of 90 days, to know you are on track to achieving your desired outcome by the end of 100 days? (Fill in the 'by the end of 90 days' box.)

Example of John, the newly appointed global head of sales of Premium Services, ABC Bank

First 100 Days Plan

'Value-adder' desired outcome: Refreshed the two-year vision for Premium Services Division and set out clear direction on next 12-month priorities.

FIRST STEPS	BY THE END OF 30 DAYS	BY THE END OF 60 DAYS	BY THE END OF 90 DAYS
• Research company vision and mission. • Understand the CEO's priorities. • Assess company performance against its vision and mission and CEO priorities.	• Existing vision and strategy fully understood. • New hypotheses developed on future requirements and next 12-month priorities. • Draft 1 of new two-year vision completed.	• Socialised new two-year vision and first 12-month priorities with key stakeholders. • Draft 2 – iterated, refined and confirmed. • Team roles and responsibilities assigned.	• Events held to launch and communicate new vision and key underpinning initiatives.

STEP 3: SENSE-CHECK AND COMPLETE YOUR FIRST 100 DAYS PLAN

By now, you should have an 11-page deck of slides as your First 100 Days Plan.

- Page 1 = your list of 10 desired outcomes to be achieved by the end of your first 100 days.

- Pages 2–11 = for every desired outcome, you should have a dedicated page showing the first steps and the 30/60/90@day breakdown as shown in Figure 2.2.

Figure 2.2 Template of your First 100 Days Plan

First 100 days plan	List of my 10 desired outcomes	Desired outcome on transition maker... First steps/By end 30/By end 60/By end 90/
	Desired outcome on content learner...	Desired outcome on business achiever...
Desired outcome on unique contributor...	Desired outcome on communications provider...	Desired outcome on relationship builder... First steps: by end of 30/60/90 days
Desired outcome on team builder...	Desired outcome on culture navigator...	Desired outcome on market player...
Desired outcome on value adder...		

More on this later, but the intention is that you will review your First 100 Days Plan at key milestones of 30 days, 60 days and 90 days to ensure that each of your 10 desired outcomes is on track throughout the 100 days. This is all about 10 key parallel activities and progressing all of them – which is why you will accelerate significantly in your role.

3

@ start

- Launch your First 100 Days Plan
- Show up as a leader, not a manager
- Bring 'sizzle' as well as substance
- EQ will be as important as IQ
- Critical success factors for the next 30 days: day 1–30

1 Launch your First 100 Days Plan

You can make a fanfare launch of your First 100 Days Plan as soon as you arrive, but my advice is not to do that. Instead, it is best to arrive and ground yourself in the role for 5 to 10 days to check what the experience is like on arrival, and to confirm and make any final tweaks to the plan.

For example, prior to arrival, you may not yet have met all the stakeholders, so your First 100 Days Plan may not have included all stakeholder expectations.

On arrival, I recommend the following steps:
- Check/reconfirm priorities with your boss and key stakeholders, and their expectations of you.
- Meet your direct report team, and get up to speed on their issues.
- Physically go into the building and organisation to get your own sense of the place.
- Finalise your First 100 Days Plan.

TO WHOM?

Whether or not to communicate your First 100 Days Plan to all role stakeholders is up to you. I recommend that you share it fully with your boss but, after that, you may choose tactically how much of the plan to share, and who with, depending on what is appropriate to your context.

AND HOW?

How you communicate your First 100 Days Plan is another matter. Whilst it was useful for you to construct your plan on paper, in terms of communication to others you may wish to avail yourself of the full suite of communication architecture available: for example, in person, roadshows, town halls, podcast, blogs, email, position paper, and/or any other effective means for your context.

2 Show up as a leader, not a manager

By now, you should feel very well prepared, your First 100 Days Plan is thorough and complete, and it is a great-looking document to discuss with your boss on arrival on Day 1. So far, so good!

But, of course, on arrival on the first day in the role, your challenge is only just beginning! You now need to bring your First 100 Days Plan to life, and execute it successfully. And so, we come full circle and refocus again not on the plan but on *you as a leader* and your ability to chart the course successfully.

We have already mentioned the word 'leader' several times so far in this book. It's time now to clarify what is meant by this over-used and misunderstood term. In my experience most business executives in major global corporations are professional managers, not leaders. You may believe you are a leader, you may have been told for years at your company that you are a leader, but I have rarely met anybody who is a real leader. Just because you are in a position of authority, this does not make you a leader.

most executives are professional managers – not 'leaders'

What I mean is that executives are relying on the power and authority of their role to get things done and, like managers, they usually take up their role as someone involved in organising and marshalling resources in servicing a task passed to them by another. That's a manager, a follower, not a leader.

Thousands of books have been written on the subject of leadership. It gets overly complicated to the extent that it feels like an impossible mission to lead anybody from point A to point B. I like to keep it simple.

A leader should:

- set a clear direction;
- bring people with him/her;
- deliver results.

In an attempt to keep it simple, I list these as the three key tasks of any leader, but please note that these are not separate tasks. These three tasks are inextricably linked and iterative and one cannot exist in isolation of the other, and this is why I use a Venn diagram as the most helpful visual to paint the picture of overlapping activity and linkages in the First100assist™ leadership framework.

Figure 3.1 First100assist™ leadership framework

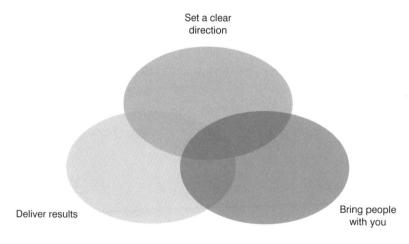

SET A CLEAR DIRECTION

No one knows the right answer about the future. But a leader will have the courage to put stakes in the ground early on and say, 'I don't have all the answers either, but let's go *there*'. 'There' could be a new market, new products and services, or a total relaunch, or all of the aforementioned. It doesn't matter what 'there' is – the leader has the guts to go for it. If 'there' is a very complicated 'point B', then you could intuitively understand that getting there will be complicated too and resistance will occur. So you have to be very clear on the direction in your first 100 days, and very clear on why you are going 'there'. The more clarity on the end point, and the plan to get to the end point, then of course the easier the journey will be for everyone to get there.

BRING PEOPLE WITH HIM/HER

Of course, if only the leader goes 'there', nothing much happens in terms of progress. The leader has to communicate his/her vision on 'there' to the people, and motivate them to journey with him/her.

Never underestimate how much you have to keep communicating your direction in the first 100 days, and the reasons for your direction, to others. Even when you don't know all the answers, keep communicating. And, of course, this is not one person trying to move a mountain, people will spontaneously follow you when they understand more about your direction and believe in you.

DELIVER RESULTS

Reaching 'there' and the attempts to get 'there' will have been a good idea and a good plan only if results prove it. Otherwise, we all realise the leader made a big mistake on direction and we were foolish to follow. The delivery of the right results demonstrates the quality of the leader in terms of ability to set a clear direction and bring the people with him/her.

That's it! In your first 100 days – and beyond – keep in mind those three leadership tasks:

- Set a clear direction on where you want to be by the end of 100 days.
- Bring your people with you (boss, team, stakeholders, customers).
- Deliver the right results by the end of the first 100 days.

3 Bring 'sizzle' as well as substance

As well as a plan ('substance'), you're going to have to have a personality ('sizzle').

In 2009 Gordon Brown was in power as Prime Minister of the UK and David Cameron was leader of the opposition. US President Barack Obama paid a visit to the UK and was asked by journalists for his opinion of both men. President Obama is said to have responded, 'Gordon Brown has substance, but David Cameron has sizzle.' If you know both men, then you know exactly what Obama meant and how his comment really hit the nail on the head! Gordon Brown knew a lot more about the finer points of economic policy, but was quite a staid communicator and he didn't relate well to the general public. Whereas, Cameron was the 'young pretender', less experienced but a lot more energetic in the way he communicated and he seemed more in touch with the concerns of modern-day society; consequently, he was a lot more appealing to the public.

I put it to you that, if you want to make the best possible impact in your first 100 days in a new role, then you need to have both sizzle *and* substance.

I don't believe that every leader has to be a stereotype of the charming, charismatic, extrovert leader, but you have to offer your followership something in the way of an 'X factor' dynamic that inspires them so that they notice you, look up to you and respect you.

you have to offer your followership something in the way of an 'X factor' dynamic

The substance of having a great First 100 Days Plan will get diluted if you cannot get people's attention, and engage and excite your people to follow it with you.

So, what do I really mean about 'sizzle' and how can you get some?!

You need to be energetic! I am talking about your ability to walk into a room in a way that people notice that you have arrived. You need to walk tall, walk purposefully, have the ability to command the attention in the room because you stride in and bring with you fresh energy. You have to have something to say, something new and different to offer – you need to have passion for what you do, and be able to convey that passion to others in terms of how you speak, your tone of voice, and what new ideas you have.

You need to be interesting to be around, and you need to be interested in other people. Do people generally want to hear what you have to say, or do you check to notice whether their eyes glaze over while you deliver overly long monologues on what all the issues and problems are? The best way to bond and engage with others is to ask them questions, and listen to their answers, and remember to pick up the conversational thread next time you meet them.

When you think about how best to create the right kind of personal impact on others, keep in mind the day-to-day presentations, the small meetings and informal encounters that occupy most of an executive's day because of how powerfully such interactions influence perceptions.

'Disclosure' can be a very powerful tactic for creating immediate and deep rapport with people on your team. For example, although you might have thought it would look like a weakness, if you admit that you are feeling daunted by the new role, then people will be more likely to empathise with you and support you for success. If you seem too aloof and too arrogant to share your challenges with them, they are less likely to support you. Winning your team's support in the first 100 days is vital for your success, so start with creating the right impression with them.

I have worked with clients who have 'sizzle' in bucket-loads. It is not even a topic that we have to cover. This is usually the case when clients have actively pursued the role and believe that they alone can make the biggest difference. This kind of confident client is driven by a mission to succeed, and their desire to be the one who can achieve substantially within the role.

However, I have also worked with clients who are a lot more passive. Through company circumstance, such as a reshuffle on high, they have been promoted into a new role for which they have no deep passion. Yes, they have the skill to do the role, and they want to do a good job – but that burning desire or connection with the role's mission does not exist. This is a much more problematic situation than they realise, because, if you don't feel fully connected with your role mission, then you lack optimal motivation and this impacts on all

find your role mission!

those around you too. After all, if you don't have the required drive and energy to lead on this role, then why would anybody on your team go the extra mile when required? You can't be half a leader – you need to be all in, or not at all.

So when I meet clients who aren't fully engaged with the mission of their role, and who are not fully engaged in their leadership of it, then I work with them to find the meaning, to ignite some passion for the job. Often, it isn't as difficult as it might sound. It usually requires some discussion about when they were younger, the reason they chose this career, and what their goals were at the time. I have found that older executives simply have forgotten much of the earlier idealism and many of the goals they had in their early career but it doesn't take long to reconnect them with those memories and persuade them to bring that kind of dynamic meaning to this role.

It is very important that executives find meaning in what they do, whether that is to make a difference in people's lives, to transform the environment, to improve society, to improve the quality of customer service, or whatever. Unsurprisingly, what you won't find is anybody below CEO level ever saying that the reason they get up in the morning is to increase shareholder value!

Now over to you:

- Why are you doing this job?
- What would make it more meaningful for you?
- How can you translate that passion for the job into extra sizzle factor to motivate others?

4 EQ will be as important as IQ

You also need to know that your EQ (emotional quotient/intellect) will be as important as your IQ (intelligence quotient/actual intellect). The analytical mindset of the executive plays tricks and creates a convenient illusion that an organisation can be controlled and managed as a set of systems, processes and organisation charts. First 100 Days Plans, whilst necessary to attempt to gain control in the first 100 days, play into this illusion – but, in the end, organisations are highly interpersonal places.

it is all about people and how they relate to each other

Whilst we emphasise the importance of having a First 100 Days Plan, we don't underestimate the importance of your EQ skills in being able to bring the plan to life with others.

EQ refers to emotional intelligence: self-awareness, self-regulation, self-motivation, empathy and social skill. Being fit for purpose on emotional intelligence will be a very important aspect of the 'how' on your First 100 Days Plan. You will need to figure out how to motivate and engage your team to deliver on the plan. To do this, you need to be aware of how you are coming across in your message (as the giver) and how the team are responding to your approach and plans.

The first 100 days is an intense time period so, naturally, your emotional reactions will be heightened. You need to have good self-awareness to observe when these heightened emotions are taking over, and you need to exercise self-regulation to manage and overcome these emotions.

For example, you may feel extremely buoyant and optimistic in the first few weeks of the first 100 days – and these feelings may exaggerate themselves to the extent that you lose touch with commercial reality and over-promise on delivery of year-end results. Your team won't thank you for this!

Or you may feel anxious at the beginning of the first 100 days – and, if you are not able to manage the anxiety, then you are more likely to postpone decision making. This will not enhance your leadership reputation, and others may lose confidence in you.

My advice is to be open to the hypothesis that no matter who you are, no matter how experienced, you will have exaggerated reactions to what is happening around you in the first 100 days of a role appointment. Be open to the idea that these emotions may range from the panic/fear/overwhelm end of the spectrum to the over-confident/arrogant end of the spectrum – and everything in-between, and that you may be in danger of 'acting out' accordingly.

The dynamic viral emotional life of the organisation will be an important factor to synthesise, diagnose and understand. For example, are your people suffering from 'change fatigue', i.e. constant changes in strategy? How can you communicate your plans in such a way that people believe in you and in what you are trying to achieve?

As leader you will be in a strong position to affect, lead and guide people towards a positive new emotional resonance if you are emotionally well equipped yourself to do so. Having the right support systems in place to sense-check both your intellectual and emotional choices will serve you well in your first 100 days.

Realise that how you handle your emotions during the first 100 days – particularly at the start – will be a critical performance acceleration make or break. Get it wrong, and you may alienate others early. Get it right, and you will make more accelerated progress.

JOHN, NEWLY APPOINTED GLOBAL HEAD OF SALES FOR PREMIUM SERVICES, ABC BANK

'Be the master of your emotions'

To date, any leadership or management training John received had been skills-based and the coach's introduction of the idea of 'emotional' intellect (EQ) being as important as actual intellect (IQ) was new to him. During this coaching session, his coach educated him on how he needed to better regulate his emotions, particularly in these early days of his new role appointment.

Coach notes from Session 3

Being aware of your own emotions is very important because of the viral effect of the leader's emotions on the rest of the team. There has been a lot of literature written regarding 'emotional intelligence' (EQ) of leaders and how EQ can be even more important than IQ (actual intellect).

You need to be a lot more aware of how everybody looks up to you as the leader. You, as leader, set the tone for all your followers. Everybody consciously or unconsciously is taking their cue from you – because you are the boss. If you are in a bad mood, literally the whole team, and the members of their teams, etc. can virally pick up on your mood and have a bad day.

Your emotions can cascade through the company via interactions with your management team, on phone calls, in meetings, in person, etc. So, it is very important that you maintain a steady state of calm emotion – because it is only when we are calm and grounded that we can truly perform to the best of our abilities. When we are calm, we are more focused and clear-headed, we make better decisions and we don't get side-tracked.

This links back to points made in our first session. Accept and deal with overwhelming feelings by introducing tactics to alleviate pressure. Also increase your self-awareness and ability to regulate your own emotions, and always attempt to maintain a calm steady state – so that you maintain your composure under pressure and so that others follow your lead. The calmer you are, the more productive you will be.

Focus on one thing at a time. When you have completed that task, let it go. Take a break. Then focus on the next thing. For example, on your recruitment issues – have you listed all the recruitment gaps, have you a plan in place on how to fill each one, is there anything else you can do to accelerate the filling of each role? If there is, do it. If there isn't, then that's it. If there is nothing more you can do on recruitment at this moment in time, then leave it in the hands of your recruitment specialists and move on to another important priority in your First 100 Days Plan. Put a process in place to ensure that your recruitment specialists update you every week – and at that designated time, ask yourself again, is there

▶

anything you can do to accelerate recruitment? If there is, do it. If not, move on.

What I am trying to say is that there is a unconscious stream of activity going on in your day where everything seems to be 'mushing' in with everything else. Try to separate out tasks, focus on one at a time, and, when you are finished, move on to the next priority task.

Prior to this, John never paid much attention to monitoring his thoughts and feelings. He never realised the effect that his moods and emotions were having on him and on all those around him, and he realised that he needed to become more familiar with the concept of 'emotional intelligence' and mastering his emotions, if he was to continue to grow as a leader and get the most out of his team.

5 Critical success factors for the next 30 days: day 1–30

Having worked with many leaders during their first 100 days, I developed a view on what were the critical success factors for personal success in the first 30 days. Now is the time to share them with you.

BRING FORWARD A CLEAR VISION

Following on from what I mentioned regarding leading versus managing, the leader in the first 100 days has to bring forward a clear vision. Even if a vision has already been set by the predecessor, I always ask clients, what is the point of having you in the job versus anybody else if you can't add, build, refresh or reinvent the vision? So, what is *your* vision? To put it another way, when you leave the role, what do you want people to say is your legacy? It's another way of starting with the end in mind – think about leaving the role, and what you want to have left behind. Then you can set out your vision.

HAVE NO FEAR (BE CONFIDENT)

I have noticed that everybody – regardless of seniority or experience – suffers a confidence loss in the first 30 days. This is natural, and I legitimise this feeling with clients. After all, they have never done this role before, so of course they would feel nervous. Confidence is very important, because you need to be able to make good decisions and not panic in the overwhelmingness of the first 100 days. Fear is the great enemy of confidence. Fear paralyses performance. But please remember that fear is only imagination about something that has not happened. Our thoughts create reality, so cancel all fear thoughts from your mind and replace them with confident thoughts. If you are gripped with fear, speak with your rational self to say that fear is just imaginary and you can choose to imagine a positive outcome instead. Another technique is to imagine a fire and, every time a fear thought comes into your mind, put it into the fire and watch it burn.

EXERCISE PATIENCE AND RESILIENCE

A leader in a new role is psyched up to perform and make changes as fast as possible, given their new authority and mandate. Unfortunately, resistance to change appears to be the status quo of even the best organisations. So, be realistic that, while you are in gung-ho mode, your team and those around you may be suffering change fatigue and may be both consciously and unconsciously resistant to your ideas. Accept that resistance to change is the more likely situation and devise strategies for overcoming these resistances. In other words, try not to get frustrated by the slow pace of others; instead, accept that it is (unfortunately) the human condition to resist change but at the same time work to overcome it. Be patient with yourself and with others. Be resilient in the face of challenges and obstacles.

BE A FAST LEARNER

The industry, market and organisation will keep on moving, and there is no pause whilst you get up to speed in the first month. So you have to be committed and able to learn as fast as possible. This is why I suggested earlier that you negotiate extra latitude and time from loved ones so that, during the first 30 days, you are fully focused on narrowing content gaps and learning the ropes as fast as possible.

DON'T BE AFRAID OF YOUR MISTAKES

We all make mistakes. That is never going to change. So don't be afraid to make mistakes – especially in the first 30 days. Mistakes are a rich source of learning and make up the sum of our total experience and wisdom. The important thing about mistakes is how you handle them – very often a mistake can be an opportunity to build a deeper relationship with someone we work with because those around you may be very forgiving of early mistakes. The only other point I would highlight is that you have to move forward with courage and without perfect information so it is inevitable that mistakes will be made – so just accept it, and don't worry about it!

part two

Middle

The nature of the middle phase: the 'middle' phase of anything is usually where the really hard work occurs.

After 30 days, the novelty of your arrival is passing, but you have not yet been there long enough to be in a position to show any results. As such, you are well and truly 'stuck in the middle'.

Everyone has expectations of you within 100 days, but your first month can fly by without anyone expecting you to do much at all. At the same time, judgement day is looming. You are a third of the way through your first 100 days, so you need to take stock and check that you are making progress and that you are on track to achieve your first 100 days desired outcomes.

the really hard work starts now

In the middle phase of your First 100 Days journey, you need to work harder, and move beyond yourself and get others working for you. 'Middle' is about staying the course and putting extra energy and effort into achieving your initiatives. The middle phase is that moment when you may feel you are up against a wall with a feeling that you may have bitten off more than you can chew. But, know that if you keep persevering, then glory awaits you. In the first 30 days you will be forgiven for spending most of your time meeting your boss, stakeholders and team and getting up to speed. But in this middle phase, that early forgiveness starts to give way to an increasing desire from your role stakeholders to see real action occurring and early results secured.

In the forthcoming chapters, I outline an approach and key steps for what you can do to tackle the two core months of your middle phase.

@ 30 days

1 Review progress against plan.

2 Decide who and what really matters here.

3 Fast-forward team performance.

4 Update your First 100 Days Plan.

5 Critical success factors for the next 30 days: day 30–60.

@ 60 days

1 Review progress against plan.

2 Make final decisions on who stays and who goes.

3 Capitalise on your leadership 'multiplier' effect.

4 Update your First 100 Days Plan.

5 Critical success factors for the next 30 days: day 60–90.

First100™ client case study continued

JOHN, NEWLY APPOINTED GLOBAL HEAD OF SALES FOR PREMIUM SERVICES, ABC BANK

'To be successful, a leader needs a high-performing team'

A month into the role, John realised the team was in even worse shape than first imagined. This was making him panic – after all, how will he get anything done by the end of his first 100 days and beyond if his team is not up to scratch?

As John booked his @ 30 days appointment with his First100™ Coach, he realised that this was the most ▶

frustrated and pressured he had felt in the role to date. He had listened to advice about how to successfully enter into the role. He had more than impressed his boss and key stakeholders from the start with a thoughtful and robust First 100 Days Plan – setting out all that he wanted to achieve within his first 100 days. Such a buoyant start had made him feel confident and in control. But, as the weeks passed, John started to realise that, if his team were not responsive or 100 per cent high performing, then all his efforts would be in vain. His early hypothesis that it would be simply a matter of empowering his team was proving naïve. In reality, they were still too dependent and lacking initiative. They agreed with every point John made about needing to be more proactive but, in reality, they didn't make any behavioural changes to back up their nodding heads. John also felt he had too many direct reports (12), and possibly only 4–6 of them were up to standard. John was starting to wonder if he needed a whole new management layer between him and his inherited team if he really was going to make his mark in this role. Perhaps his coach would have some answers ...

Interestingly, the coach said she had heard it all before. She told him that it may be news to John that he was disappointed in his inherited team, but really this was a very common experience when newly appointed leaders assessed the quality of their team members. According to the coach's experience, the quality of leadership in organisations is often poor and, consequently, the quality of teams in organisations is also poor.

What the coach also knew is that the newly appointed

leader vacillates on this point of 'fixing' the team. Time and time again, she said, she listened to leaders explaining how they are not happy with their team – but as soon as she suggested they do something about it, there were always the usual excuses that it was too soon, or it wouldn't look good, or people needed to be given a chance, etc. And very often, at the end of the first 100 days, leaders still were complaining about their team – and still not doing anything constructive about it.

She urged John to tackle the issue head on, and make changes in the team as quickly as possible, and to accelerate new recruitment plans to get fresh talent on board – either from elsewhere in the organisation and/or from external hiring. She gave John the confidence to do so, by discussing her experiences, and by forcing him to confront the issue of how can a leader achieve anything without a proper team.

> *Firstly, look at the way the team is structured and empower yourself to change it. Don't necessarily add new layers, as this may be fudging the issue and creating too much middle management. Step back from the team itself, and think about what you want to achieve within the role in two years. By focusing on the two-year desired outcomes, what are the roles you need people to fulfil? Don't think about existing roles or role titles, suspend any tendencies to think that things have to be the way they are – instead, break free and think about how to craft new roles and responsibilities in line with your two-year desired outcomes and the skills and motivations of the people on your team.*

4

@ 30 days

- ● Review progress against plan
- ● Decide who and what really matters here
- ● Fast-forward team performance
- ● Update your First 100 Days Plan
- ● Critical success factors for the next 30 days: day 30–60

1 Review progress against plan

Review progress against plan

@ 30 DAYS

1 Review your desired outcomes for the first 100 days.

2 Are you on track to achieve those desired outcomes?

3 Are you where you expected to be @ 30 days?

4 Take stock of what is working well/not well with your plan @ 30 days:
  - What more can you do to improve your performance against plan?
  - Brainstorm solutions to any blocks/challenges
  - Think about the performance acceleration opportunities
  - Who can help you with this exercise and act as sounding board/coach?

The most important thing to do right now is to stop, take stock and review progress against where you expected to be 30 days into your First 100 Days Plan. We all know you have been busy, but have you been busy doing the right things?

Since arriving, no doubt external factors have kicked in, or the situation is worse/different/better than envisaged. Stay focused on your plan. Derailment from the strategic priorities is what stops executives making maximum impact in the first 100 days.

are you busy-good or busy-bad?

This @ 30 day mark represents a key milestone opportunity to take stock of progress and check whether you have fallen into the trap of low-level detail, 'fire-fighting' or other distractions.

Take out your First 100 Days Plan and set aside at least two hours for a serious review:

- Are you staying focused on your key priorities?
- Have you achieved what you wanted by this point, in service of your desired outcomes by the end of the first 100 days? What are you spending time on?
- If you are spending time on activities not on the plan, then ask yourself, why? You either adjust the plan or stop doing them.
- Use the following @ 30 days checklist to reflect back on the last 30 days.

@ 30 days checklist

1 How did you spend your own time and energy in the first 30 days?

You cannot do everything, but making the right choices on how you spend your time, day to day, at different stages in the first 100 days will be important – in both symbolic and real terms. For example, how much time did you spend in the last 30 days talking with your customers? How much time did you spend out in the field understanding how the sales force works versus sitting in an office locked away from the 'real world'? How much time have you invested with your team versus constantly trying to please your boss? In your first 30 days, what you are spending time on, or – perhaps even more importantly – what you are perceived to be spending your time on, will be noticed by others. You can use this insight more consciously by deliberately choosing how you spend your time, so that it symbolically re-enforces your

▶

First 100 Days priorities, showing others that you 'walk the talk', and this gives them the motivation to act accordingly. It is also very real because, if you are a person of substance and if you invest time and attention in a particular area, then it should reap a tangible measurable dividend because of your focus and involvement.

2 Did you manage the overwhelmingness, and rise above the sea of well wishers?

During the first 30 days, you will have a lot of new people to meet, and to deal with – both externally and internally. Everybody wants a 'piece' of you, and that can be overwhelming. Your ability to judge who is valuable, who is authentic, who is reliable, who can deliver, will be crucial in accelerating First 100 Days priorities and plans. Some of my clients have told me that, on arrival, they receive hundreds of emails in their first week and they have no idea how to prioritise them and how to respond, because they don't know yet who is important and who are the time-wasters. My suggestion is to keep it simple and straightforward – be pleasant and friendly to everyone. Smile at everyone, shake hands when appropriate, reply to emails, even if only with a brief stock reply like, 'Thank you so much for getting in touch. I would like to meet up as soon as I figure out my schedule.' An email like this is good because, firstly, you are acknowledging respect to the sender by replying and not ignoring them, secondly, it starts with a thank you (always nice) and, finally, it buys you some time as you find out whether this person is important to meet (you can ask your boss and/or your trusted team members). It is the kind of email that won't have repercussions if you don't follow up, because there is an implied message that you have a lot going on.

3 How did you deal with your predecessor?

How you deal with your predecessor in the first 30 days will be important and will send signals as to how you deal with people. Regardless of whether your predecessor did a good job or not, the respectful thing to do is to thank them publicly and then take over.

Bizarrely I see a common number of cases where the predecessor has not gone away at all! The newly appointed leader arrives to find that his predecessor, who failed to succeed in the job, has somehow successfully influenced (or, through guilt, convinced) the boss into believing it is for your benefit that he should stay around and do a one-three- or six(!)-month handover. If this is the case with you, be strong and explain that two people cannot be in charge at one time and that it will be confusing for the team if their old boss is still in place whilst you come in with new ideas on how to change things. Explain that, naturally, your predecessor will not like any of your new suggestions, and will likely take any criticism personally, so thank your boss for the offer but give a definite 'No thank you' and suggest that your predecessor works on a specific helpful initiative from the comfort of their home until a new role is found for them. This forces the issue for the organisation on what to do with your predecessor, and means that you are free to get on with your job.

4 How did you respond to first mistakes/bad news/ early pressure?

It's a bit like an early courtship in the first 30 days.

▶

As such, everybody wants to please and impress everybody else. But, being humans, it is inevitable that mistakes will be made and that misunderstandings will arise. You are new to the role and you will make mistakes. Your people will also make mistakes. No matter how experienced the CEO and the top team, wrong turns are inevitable. So, accept that this is inevitable and develop a method for how you respond to mistakes – made by you, or by others. How you recover from wrong turns, how you handle yourself and others during the heightened stress period of the first 100 days will be important. Having a set of 'pressure-valve-release' systems in place, such as those described in the 'Energy management section' earlier, can be crucial for staying centred and keeping in perspective any early mistakes made.

5 **How well have you coped with the unknowns and avoided derailment?**

It is quite normal that a First 100 Days Plan doesn't have contingency for unknowns – given that unknowns are obviously hard to cater for in a plan! For example, macro external factors may come more into play. And/or more micro issues may come into play, especially on arrival and during the first 30 days. You need to be adaptable, of course, but you need to find the right balance between being adaptable versus being too reactive. It is unlikely that any unknowns are so striking as to change your whole First 100 Days Plan – unless, for example, your company announces bankruptcy! – so 9.5 times out of 10 you need to subsume new information into your plan, rather than completely overhaul it. If your First 100 Days Plan has been written with the strategic end in mind, then it is unlikely that the desired outcomes would need to change – however, be prepared to adjust the actions needed to achieve those outcomes.

6 Have you a sense as to whether you have the right people in the right roles?

Having explained the 'what' you want to achieve to your people, perhaps they will struggle on the 'how'. Having smart, driven, agile people around you will be very important. It may take a disproportionate amount of time upfront in the first 100 days to realise who really is on the bus with you – and you will need to continue to sense-check it from time to time. Now that you are a month in, take stock and think about the people you have inherited and their skill set and their potential development under your leadership. More on this later in the chapter, as building a high-performing team is crucial to your success.

7 How well are you communicating your First 100 Days Plan?

How you communicate your plan will make or break the mobilisation of others in terms of delivering the plan. You may need to find several ways of saying the same thing. Installing and leveraging the right breadth and depth of 'communication architecture' is a critical area of importance for First 100 Day success. By the end of 30 days, 'your' plan needs to become 'our' plan as far as your team and role stakeholders are concerned. There is no point in having a great plan of your own if no one else bought into it. It could be the best First 100 Days Plan in the world but, if nobody knows about it, it may as well not exist. There are so many new ways of communicating, beyond dry PowerPoint, so take advantage of new social media to reach out and connect with people at all levels of your organisation.

8 **How aligned are you with your boss and your boss's boss?**

Alignment with your boss is very important, of course, but don't necessarily limit the definition of boss to the obvious. Perhaps your immediate boss is out of step or out of favour, so make sure you also meet your boss's boss – just to check their alignment, and to get a heads up regarding what discussions are taking place further up the leadership 'food chain' on strategic challenges facing the company.

9 **Are you celebrating your successes and having fun along the way?**

Your first 100 days will be intense, so it is very important to factor in time for pausing, taking stock, celebrating successes on the journey. The first 100 days is like a sprint and the rest of the first 12 months is like a marathon. At both stages, but particularly in the sprint stage, you will want to ensure that you feel fulfilled throughout the whole experience so that it is both energetic and energising.

2 Decide who and what really matters here

With 30 days' experience under your belt, now is a good time to ask yourself:

- What really matters here?
- Who really matters here?

It takes time to work these nuances out. And that's why I'm bringing this up now – you have been busy getting started in the last 30 days, but now is the time to lift up your head again and think more deeply about these points.

Culture and politics are an integral part of organisational life. Naturally, you may have been briefed on what matters in this role and in this organisation, prior to joining, but I suggest you make up your own mind, based on your experience of having been in the role for a month.

Skilled political behaviour involves understanding how organisations work and mobilising resources to achieve the organisation's purposes. High-achieving leaders realise that there are two dimensions at play in every relationship, every meeting, every department, every organisation: what is happening 'above the surface' and what is happening 'below the surface'. The ability to read the organisational world is a very important skill, and you may have the greatest First 100 Days Plan in the world, but, if you miss out on *what really matters here*, then all your efforts will be in vain.

- Do you know how the organisation works, its processes, procedures, systems?
- Do you have a feel for the power bases, overt and covert agendas, formal and informal networks?
- Who are the key decision makers and influencers?
- Do you understand the formal organisation chart and the informal organisation chart?
- What needs to be read is usually not formally explained or written down, so are you politically aware enough to read between the lines?
- If you are not politically savvy, then how are you going to mitigate this?

**check below
the surface –
how does this
company really
work?**
Reading an organisation takes skill, time and sensitivity to other people. You need to get good at reading the political structure of the organisation and what makes it tick. Invest in the network now. Don't just focus on the delivery task at hand; my suggestion is that you reach out and invest time on understanding important relationships and networks too. Time spent building goodwill relationships now will prove invaluable in getting things done faster later on. If asked, perhaps your boss or human resources department can help assign you an internal mentor. Ideally, select a wise mentor who has been in the company for years, has survived organisation restructures and a change of one or more CEOs, and is prepared to help you read the corporate culture and help you to get up to speed on corporate politics as soon as possible.

3 Fast-forward team performance

In the first 30 days, the attention has been on you, but a leader cannot achieve anything without a strong, high-performing team.

Frankly, you cannot underestimate the importance of getting this right. One of the great advantages of being a newly appointed leader is that you have a window of opportunity whereby you have automatic permission to change things and to challenge the status quo. In fact, you are expected to make changes to the team – everybody knows this, but the team will be sending you resistance signals and telling you that it is not the right time because, of course, people are inherently afraid of change. But the longer you are there in the role, without making changes to the team, the harder it will be to justify later on why you were happy with the team for months and then suddenly want to make changes. So, take advantage now to make your most radical moves, and do it as swiftly as possible!

I have found it works to think of the team using the analogy of the body; and within this frame, a team is considered healthy (i.e. high-performing) if the sum of the parts is a clear head (team analytics, team intelligence, team knowledge), capable hands (team skills, team competencies), and a strong heart (team passion, team motivation, team spirit). I put it to you that each component part of the 'body' must be in place in order for the whole to function effectively.

build the health of your team

Time for a health-check

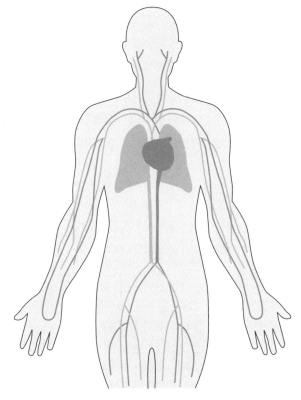

Step back and do a health check on your team. Does the sum of the parts make up a healthy team? For example, does the team have the intelligence (head), the skills (hands), but lack the passion (heart) for high performance?

Ideas for building the health of your team may include:

- investing in skills training;
- investing in team building;
- recruiting to fill the gaps.

If the previous insight was about the sum of the parts, we suggest you also examine the individual parts.

do you have the right people in the right roles?

By now, one month into your new role, you have a lot more personal experience and information on what needs to be achieved, the likely challenges ahead, and the quality of the team around you.

- Do you have the right people in the right roles?
- What changes need to be made now or need to be planned for later?
- What, if anything, is missing in the context of the goals you want to achieve?
- Do you need to bring fresh talent and energy from elsewhere in the organisation or hire externally?

And the answer to the latter question is always a resounding 'yes'.

Yes, you have to give your inherited people a chance, but moving too slowly on putting the right people in the right roles can have a very negative impact on performance acceleration in the first 100 days and the first 12 months.

4 Update your First 100 Days Plan

Update your First 100 Days Plan
@ 30 days

1 Review each desired outcome and reset the actions for
   the next 30 days, based on your first 30 days' experience,
   and on:
   – A review of progress against plan

   – A sense-check using the @ 30 days checklist

   – An analysis of 'who and what matters here'

▶

- New ideas and opportunities on how to 'fast-forward team performance'

5 Critical success factors for the next 30 days: day 30–60

The following is a summary of what you should be thinking about in your next 30 days.

BE REALISTIC ABOUT THE PROBLEMS

There is no point in holding on to any (preferred) illusion that everything is perfect. After the initial high of your promotion, and the adrenalin rush of starting the role, it is now time to fully open up your eyes to the problems and challenges that you are experiencing on the ground. Usually during days 30 to 60, there is a dawning realisation by the newly appointed executive that things are even worse than expected – perhaps he notices that his boss is more of a bully than the nice guy he portrayed himself as at interview stage, or he notices that the team are slackers or that the CEO is too self-serving and not really focused on improving the company. Naturally, when this dawning or these kinds of realisations set in, the greatest temptation is to resist and ignore them – because you would rather hold on to the idea that everything is better than your last company, or your last job, and any suggestion otherwise means that denial is more preferable than acceptance. My advice is that, if you want to achieve accelerated success in your first 100 days, acceptance of the deeper problems you are facing in this situation is more preferable and more constructive than denial.

TAKE ADVANTAGE OF YOUR NEWNESS

There is a window of opportunity during days 30 to 60 to start to make some radical changes. Perhaps in the first 30 days you did not have enough information – or, even if you did, it may have seemed premature to others to immediately make changes as soon as you arrived. However, during this next month, it is perfect timing to be able to say that you have been in the role for a month and that you have a deeper understanding of the issues and the necessary changes. When you initially did your profiling of the role, organisation, market perhaps you formed some early hypotheses on what needed fixing or changing. Having been in the role for 30 days, you now have the permission to support those hypotheses via your personal observations and experiences. Don't let this opportunity pass you by. Getting the balance right of when to make changes, and when you have enough rationale for making changes, the better – as you will be seen to have courage to push forward changes sooner than expected, but not so soon as to be seen to be arrogant or un-informed.

INVEST IN THE NETWORK NOW

By definition, you can't be a successful leader unless you have some followers. Your team have little choice but to do what you say – because you are their boss, and you have control over their performance appraisals and their pay – but today's corporations are so highly matrixed that it is unlikely you have direct authority over most of the people you rely on to get things done. So, with the galaxy matrix of your organisation, how you navigate your network and secure followers will be vital to your success and it is something that you can think about during the next 30 days. You have been in the role long enough to have got some sense of the network within which you have to operate. Invest in the network now, and find ways to create rapport with and followers among the people who can help you to get things done. Don't be afraid to reach out beyond your immediate division – people will respect you more if you invest time in trying to understand what happens in the field or in the customer store or wherever your end consumer experiences your product or service.

GET OUT OF THE OFFICE

It is understandable that you may have had to spend the first 30 days in the office, meeting your boss and your team and establishing yourself in your role. However, don't let another month go by without getting out of your immediate office block. Visit your group headquarters, your customers, the competition, your key suppliers – get out of your office to get some more perspective. At a minimum, you will learn more and will be seen to be more hands on and less 'ivory tower'. At a maximum, you might discover innovations or new solutions that unlock your current issues.

BE THE BEST LEADER YOU CAN BE

You need to check in with yourself, in the next 30 days, to make sure you are being the best leader you can be. Are you setting a clear direction, are you bringing people with you, are you getting the right results? The @ 90 day milestone is the best stage to gather formal feedback – more on this later! – but, in the meantime, take opportunities to informally check in with your boss and your team on how your leadership messages are being received and if you are gaining some followers and momentum on achieving the right results expected of you.

5

@ **60 days**

- Review progress against plan
- Make final decisions on who stays and who goes
- Capitalise on your leadership 'multiplier' effect
- Update your First 100 Days Plan
- Critical success factors for the next 30 days: day 60–90

1 Review progress against plan

Review progress against plan
@ 60 days

1 Review your desired outcomes for the first 100 days.

2 Are you on track to achieve those desired outcomes?

3 Are you where you expected to be @ 60 days?

4 Take stock of what is working well/not well with your
plan @ 60 days.
  - What more can you do to improve your performance
    against plan?
  - Brainstorm solutions to any blocks/challenges
  - Think about the performance acceleration opportunities
  - Who can help you with this exercise, and act as
    sounding board/coach?

The most important thing to do right now is to stop, take stock, and review progress against where you expected to be 60 days into your First 100 Days Plan. We all know you have been busy, but have you been busy doing the right things?

The first 100 days is intense, and the middle phase is tiring as you get to grips with the detail of the role. It is time to regroup and reset your energy levels, and get ready for the final surge.

You are now two months in and, of course, new external factors will have kicked in, or the situation is worse/different/better than envisaged. Stay focused on your **the end of your first 100 days is in sight, so go for it** plan. Derailment from the strategic priorities is what stops executives making an impact in the first 100 days. This @ 60 days mark represents a key milestone opportunity to take stock of progress and check whether you have fallen into the trap of low-level detail or 'fire-fighting' or other distractions. It's time to dust off your plan – especially if you haven't looked at it in a while!

Take out your First 100 Days Plan and set aside at least two hours for a serious review.

- Are you staying focused on your key priorities?
- Have you achieved what you wanted by this point, in service of your desired outcomes by the end of the first 100 days? What are you spending time on?
- If you are spending time on activities not on the plan, then ask yourself, why? You either adjust the plan or stop doing them.
- Use the following @ 60 days checklist to reflect back on the last 30 days.

@ 60 days checklist

1   Have you met all your key stakeholders yet?
You have been in your new role for two months and it is time to check whether you have met all your key role stakeholders yet. If much more time goes by, and you have not met all the critical players, then, at a minimum, it will be seen as bad manners, but, at worst, you may not have all the information you need regarding how to be successful in this role, and what is expected from you. So, take stock, and find the time in your diary to cover all remaining stakeholder visits and meetings between now and the end of your first 100 days.

2   Are you up to speed on your CEO's priorities? Do you have a sense of the company mission?

You will be seen as a much more mature leader if you continuously keep track of CEO priorities and what is taking place at the group executive leadership meetings. Typically, there is a monthly letter or blog published by the CEO office in every corporation – it takes less than five minutes to read but it is worth linking in with it, to stay abreast of what is being discussed at the top table. For example, if there is a renewed commitment to being more socially conscious, then that might inspire you to introduce a corporate social responsibility initiative within your division – and this might be great for team bonding and help connect your team with the top leadership team.

3   Are you getting the pace right?

If you have reached the @ 60 days mark, then you have been through an intense time. Do you feel tired, overwhelmed, in need of a short break in order to regain perspective? Alternatively, if you don't feel stretched, why not? Could you ratchet up a gear, so that you make more of an effort for the final stages of your first 100 days? Just because nobody else is pushing you does not mean that people will be any less judgemental if you don't produce results by the end of your first 100 days. Or perhaps, in your organisation, everyone more or less gets a 'free ride' for the first 12 months? If the pace of your corporation is slow, then it will be even more important for you to have an accelerated start so that you can continue to set yourself apart from others and ensure fast-track leadership promotions.

4 Are you on track to deliver real results?

If I were to bump into you in the corridor of your offices, could you convince me that you are on track to deliver tangible results? I am sure you are doing a lot of 'stuff', but how sure can you be that any of it will result in tangible deliverables that you can be proud of at the end of your first 100 days? So, take a moment to ask yourself – are you on track to deliver a real result, such as *x* per cent uplift in sales, or a physical document such as the marketing plan, or phase 1 results from a newly launched strategic initiative? Be your own harshest critic and, if your activities are not yet grounded in a tangible deliverable, then think about how you can convert your efforts into a document, a presentation or something 'physical' that can be used to show others the quantitative and qualitative progress that you are making.

5 How well are you dealing with your people issues?

What is your view on your direct report team? Are they a motivated, high-performing group – or do they fall way below your expectations of the required standard? Do you have an action plan in place to improve the performance of your direct report team – what initiatives are you going to launch to make the most of what you have got, even if you also have external recruitment plans under way to refresh the team?

6 Do you have the necessary budget and resources?

Have you secured the budget and resources required to make the kind of impact and change necessary to deliver not only on your first 100 days, but also on

▶

your first 12-month priorities and your two-year role vision?

7   How many mistakes have you made to date?
If you can't list at least five mistakes, then you are not self-aware and you may want to close the gap on your blind spots very quickly by soliciting the views of others as to what mistakes have been made and how they can now be rectified.

8   Are you looking after your health and energy levels?
Remember way back in Chapter 1 on preparing for your first 100 days during the pre-start phase? Go back and refresh your memory on the energy management system and take the necessary actions to maintain/regain increased energy for the final surge of the next 30–40 days.

9   Have you generated any new role insights?
You have been in this role for 60 days now. You have a lot more information and experience about this role, the main players, the market, and what can realistically be achieved. You are well positioned at this @ 60 days stage to step back and generate fresh insights on leapfrog moves or strategic innovations that can transform how you go to market.

10 Are you and your boss aligned?
Ideally, you and your boss should be at one in terms of what needs to be achieved and how. Or even if you differ on approach, you at least need to agree on what needs to be achieved in terms of direction. It is important to check in regularly with your boss during your first 100 days, as s/he is your primary advocate, if s/he made the decision to appoint you. Your

boss's success and your success, and vice versa, are inextricably linked, so the more you guys are aligned and bonding well, the better for you and your first 100 days' success.

First100™ client case study

JOHN, NEWLY APPOINTED GLOBAL HEAD OF SALES FOR PREMIUM SERVICES, ABC BANK

'Let's remind ourselves, what exactly is Leadership?'
John was now two months into his new role. He felt he had made a lot of progress, and was well and truly involved in the reality of his role. It wasn't exactly how he thought it would be – it was harder! – but a certain number of things he had been working on were beginning to come together and bear fruit, such as how to manage his key stakeholders, how to organise his team, and how to communicate to his wider community of people. Most crucially, John felt grounded and aware of the challenges, and his confidence was growing.

On reflection, perhaps he entered his @ 60 days session feeling a bit too smug, because his coach took him right back to basics – to remind him again what leadership is all about.

Coach notes from Session 5

Remember, John, the word 'leadership' is an over-used and much misunderstood term, perhaps like the word 'parent'. For example, you can become a 'parent' simply by having children – but this doesn't mean you are a good parent. And it doesn't mean that you are all set and have nothing to learn. Everyone in a position of leadership thinks they are a 'leader' and yet I have never met a real leader of the standard that I would expect from someone in charge. Just because you are in a position of authority, and you are getting things done, it does not mean you are a good leader.

You are a good leader, if you are able to consistently:

- set a clear direction;
- bring people with you;
- get the right results.

What do I mean by 'Set a clear direction'?

Does everybody in your organisation understand the company vision, the business strategy, the first and next steps in relation to their role and contribution? (Are any of these even in place?)

What do I mean by 'Bring people with you'?

Do people follow you because they have to, because they are afraid of losing their jobs and/or because they are like sheep with no independent thought or challenge, or because they deeply trust and respect you to take them in the right direction?

What do I mean by 'Get the right results'?

Was the direction right, were people right to follow you? We only know this once we see that you can get the right results. No point in setting off on a path, and

> *persuading others to follow, if it means everybody ends up in the wrong place, with the wrong results.*
>
> As John put the coach notes away, he remembered the closing remarks his coach made as he left the room:
>
> *'Remember that being a good leader is a constant commitment and journey. You're never done.'*

2 Make final decisions on who stays and who goes

By now, you have two months' experience of your team's performance. Under the 'Team builder' section of your First 100 Days Plan, you may have already reorganised the team structure, reassigned roles and responsibilities, and you may even have moved some people on and brought in fresh new talent.

However, 60 days can go by in a flash and sometimes these tough people decisions have not been taken yet. Or, it may be the case that some decisions have been taken but not *all* decisions have been taken yet.

now is the time to decide who stays and who goes

I suggest that now, in the spirit of moving quickly to achieve your aims, it is time to make any final lingering decisions on who stays/who goes.

Remind yourself of your role mission, and what you want to

achieve within two years, and how important it is in that context to get off to an accelerated start. You have to have the right team in place with everybody rowing in the right direction, and everybody a fully signed up contributing member of the team.

With that in mind, consider again your team – and in particular, your direct report team. Consider their skills, experience and added value, and their potential.

Can you spot the person who is not a net contributor? i.e. the person who is consuming more value than they are contributing, and with whom, realistically, no level of skills-building or investment is going to give you the fast high net return that you require from a high-performing team member.

Nobody likes to let people go, but avoiding the issue is hardly helpful either. It makes you look weak, and can affect the overall motivation of other team members. Eventually you will have to make these tough personnel decisions, and it is better to make them early on.

Although I work with very senior executives, who think of themselves as hard-nosed business-minded leaders, these tough people calls seem to linger on and on. Unfortunately, I am no longer ever surprised when the non-net-contributor is still in place, not just after the first 100 days, but even 12 months later.

Do yourself and that person a favour – make your decision now on who stays and who goes.

3 Capitalise on your leadership 'multiplier' effect

You now have 60 days' track record in the role, and people will be watching you and paying attention to what you do and what you say. Followers consciously and unconsciously mirror and copy the behaviours of the leader and now is the time that you can really capitalise on what I call the leadership 'multiplier' effect, to create a ripple effect on positive behaviours in others and a ripple effect of positive emotions in others – all of which will improve the morale, motivation and performance of your team and those around you.

By definition, a leader has followers. So, if all those working for you consciously or unconsciously will follow your lead, and everyone working for them will follow their lead, and so on, then the cascading effect is extremely powerful as a change mechanism and it starts with you! Take charge of this multiplier effect, and work it to your advantage.

As the leader of the team, your multiplier effect can be both positive and negative. You are already demonstrating positive behaviours that come naturally to you – but what about your negative behaviours? Unfortunately, all your negative traits are also being copied, multiplying and cascading and causing problems. So, as a leader, you need to pay attention to changing your negative behaviours.

Identify an insight on where one of your worst behaviours is having an impact on the performance of your First 100 Days Plan and decide to change it.

For example, it could be that you don't pay attention to the morale of your team, and so you now decide to let your team know that you feel this is an area you have neglected and now you want to be more thoughtful and more open to ideas from them on how to improve team morale.

If you focus on changing one thing about yourself – a quality, a characteristic, a standard, behaviour, or a norm – it has a multiplier effect on all those around you.

if a team is like a 'soup', remember you have the strongest flavour

If we think about this in relation to our earlier section on emotional intelligence, then think about how you can create what is known as 'positive resonance', i.e. deliberately create positive emotions in your team.

As the leader, you have the most 'flavour' or the most 'seasoning' in your team 'soup' – and you can decide what that flavour is, and how strong it can be. For example, if you and your team have had a recent market success, then you can use that to consciously exploit the 'feel-good factor' of the success, and press coverage to sustain employee morale and motivation for *as long as possible*. Everybody wants to feel like they are part of something important and exciting. Everybody's motivation will soar if they feel that they are part of a winning team – so celebrate all your early wins and make every team member and every recent recruit feel part of that celebration.

4 Update your First 100 Days Plan

Update your First 100 Days Plan
@ 60 days

Review each desired outcome and reset the actions for
the next 30 days, based on your first 60 days' experience,
and on:

- A review of progress against plan

- A sense-check using the @ 60 days checklist

- An analysis of 'make final decisions on who stays and
  who goes'

- New ideas and opportunities on how to 'capitalise on
  your leadership multiplier effect'

5 Critical success factors for the next 30 days: day 60–90

The following is a summary of what you should be thinking about in your next 30 days.

REFOCUS AND RESURGE

If you think all the hard work is behind you, think again! The next 30 days are what it is all about. This month it is all about 'extra energy in = exponential energy out', i.e. the more energy you put into your work during this month, the more reward you will reap. You are at that very special tipping point now where you should have enough basic information and experience of the company that any further traction should be exponentially better for the next 30 days – so go for it!

GET THE TEAM WORKING FOR YOU

In the next 30 days, your team needs to work hard to support you. Get your team working effectively, as individuals and as a team. Perhaps your team needs its own First 100 Days Plan now – which is an exercise you or a First100™ Coach can take them through – which is focused on what they want to achieve in the next 100 days. This is an opportunity for a shared mission, for more team-bonding and more team focus.

BOND WITH YOUR PEOPLE

For the past 60 days, your interactions with people have, likely, mainly been about simply 'meeting and greeting' people – surface introductions and surface-level interactions. Go deeper, now, on improving your working relationships. Try to consciously 'bond' more deeply now with the people around you. By this, I mean disclose more, listen more, invest more time, take the relationship to the next level. I am not saying you need to be someone you are not – or that you need to be everybody's friend – but what I am saying is find your own way of taking your working relationships to the next level. In effect, it will help you bond more closely with the organisation, and lead to more fulfilment at work – and, if you're a new external hire, you will start to feel less isolated and less like a 'newbie'.

REASSURE YOURSELF THAT 'YES, YOU ARE DOING A GOOD JOB'

Talking to yourself – sounds like a strange thing to advise?! – well, in my experience, executives are very insecure in their first 100 days and they need a lot of reassurance, but they don't ask for it. If they don't ask, and if they don't spontaneously get regular reassurance and validation from others, then they may act out their anxiety in all sorts of unhelpful ways – including too much arrogance and too much self-praise. Don't be one of those people. Change the game – find ways of reassuring yourself that you are making progress, so that you don't have to constantly rely on positive stroking from others or constantly speak about your progress with a hidden question mark at the end of every sentence!

START TO RECORD YOUR PROGRESS AND LESSONS LEARNED

This middle section is often where the really good progress occurs. It is a good idea to write it down and record such progress, any lessons learned and any key insights. At the end of your 100 days, I recommend that you formally present a record of your First

100 Days achievements to your boss and key stakeholders, but it is worth making notes now because you will be amazed at how much you have already learned and your whole First 100 Days journey should be reflected at day 100 – not just the progress made in the last 10 days.

part three

End

Psychologists say that endings are always psychologically painful, whether people are consciously aware of it or not. Taoists wisely say every ending is simply a new beginning. When it comes to arriving at the end phase of your first 100 days, what I say to you is that you need to enjoy a positive ending and get ready to write your 'Second Act' (more on this later!). You have been around long enough now for people to have formed a view of you – it is time to sense-check that view and see it as valuable information for a reflection on your First 100 Days leadership impact. Reflect back to extract and learn lessons from the experience. Celebrate the wins, mourn the missed opportunities, and then draw a line under it.

enjoy a positive ending!

In the next two chapters, I outline an approach and key steps for what you can do to tackle the final stages of your first 100 days and how to move forward into a whole new phase: the start of the rest of your first 12 months in the role.

@ 90 days

1   Review progress against plan.

2   Write your 10-day 'to-do' list.

3   Ask for feedback.

4   Take time out for self-reflection.

5   Critical success factors for the final 10 days: day 90–100.

End

1   Close out your First 100 Days Plan.

2   Record achievements and capture lessons learned.

3   Communicate First 100 Days success to stakeholders.

4   Celebrate with your team.

5   Consider your 'Second Act'.

6

@ 90 days

- Review progress against plan

- Write your 10-day 'to-do' list

- Ask for feedback

- Take time out for self-reflection

- Critical success factors for the final 10 days: day 90–100

1 Review progress against plan

Review progress against plan
@ 90 days

1 Review your desired outcomes for the first 100 days.

2 Are you on track to achieving those desired outcomes?

3 Are you where you expected to be @ 90 days?

4 Take stock on what is working well/not well with your plan @ 90 days.

You have only 10 days left ... so now what?!

Take out your First 100 Days Plan and set aside at least two hours for a serious review.

● Are you staying focused on your key priorities?
● Have you achieved what you wanted by this point, in service of your desired outcomes by the end of the first 100 days? What are you spending time on?

- If you are spending time on activities not on the plan, then ask yourself, why? You either adjust the plan or stop doing them.

- Use the following @ 90 days checklist to reflect back, not just on the last 30 days, but on the last 90 days.

You now have 10 days left to tidy up and bring your First 100 Days Plan to a successful close.

- Have you achieved some/all/none of your desired outcomes?

- What can you do in the next two weeks to draw a line under certain phases of activity and be able to demonstrate progress, and to ensure you have something to say about your first 100-day record of achievements?

@ 90 days checklist

1   Have you achieved everything you set out to achieve?
At the beginning of your first 100 days, you had a set of challenges to overcome and a set of desired outcomes to achieve. How has your record over the past 90 days stacked up against your aspirations and efforts? Even if you have had the most difficult of transitions, you will have made some sort of progress over the last three months, so take time to appreciate and record all your positive achievements.

2   Have you laid the foundations for the rest of your first 12 months in office?
Remember, the whole point of having an accelerated start is so that you lay the right foundations for a successful first 12 months and beyond. Are you satisfied that you have done all you can to achieve

▶

this, and what could you do in the next 10 days to really nail it? A good start is half the battle and, if you have been strategic, then the foundations built in your first 100 days will have set you up for accelerated success in your first 12 months.

3 Are your stakeholders satisfied with your performance?

Do you know what people's perceptions are of you, at this early stage – i.e. your boss, your peers, your direct reports, your wider team and your key customers? The next 10 days are an opportunity to gather feedback formally and informally, and people will be very impressed with you if you are open enough to ask them for feedback – and it will also remind people that you have only been here for three months, which will give them cause for appreciation of all the positive achievements, and pause for 'forgiveness' for any lack of progress or early mistakes and cultural gaffes.

4 Does your team respect you?

It is faster and easier to get your team to work harder if they like and – more importantly – respect you. Your team will respect you if they believe that you are adding value as their new leader, and if the team is performing better under your leadership. The question of whether they respect you may be difficult for you to answer, but start with examining your own attitude to this question – as the 'new guy' are you trying too hard to be liked, when really you should be focused on being a strong leader and doing the right thing, even if that requires making tough decisions that affect the people around you?

5   Has the market heard from you?

Was there a formal role announcement to the marketplace at the beginning of your first 100 days to signal the importance of your role and that you are now in charge of that role? Now is the optimal time to prepare another press release talking about what you have achieved in your first 100 days. More importantly, 'has your market heard from you' in the sense of whether you have delivered a win into your marketplace that benefits your customers or means you have impacted your industry dynamics?

6   Can you list your quick wins – both qualitative and quantitative?

What have been the key wins since the beginning of your first 100 days? This could be anything from the recruitment of a key strategic hire to early delivery of £ results to improved % customer retention, etc. Every success is important and it can be very reassuring to start to list them at this stage. In the forthcoming chapter, I offer you a suggested template that you can use to make a record of your achievements, with the intention of presenting them to your boss and key stakeholders at the end of your first 100 days.

7   How would you rate your own performance?

Put aside getting the positioning right with others for a moment and have an honest moment of self-reflection – how would you rate your own performance in the last 90 days? In the end, only you can really rate the effort you have put into this new role, and the real progress you have made. What have you done well, and what have you not done well? If

▶

you cannot list all your mistakes as easily as you can list all the great achievements, then you are not yet a mature and confident leader.

8   How does your boss rate your performance?

What signals, positive or otherwise, is your boss sending out to you and to others in terms of how they rate your performance? How supportive are they? Do you need to make any final requests on your boss's time or services as you wrap up on the final 10 days of your first 100 days?

9   What have your learned from the whole experience?

Take time out to think about what you have learned about yourself, your role, your organisation, your market. What do you now know, that you didn't know at the beginning of your first 100 days? If you have been running fast, and haven't had much time for reflection, then the time for that is the next 10 days. Try to balance out the hectic activity of that last 90 days with space for productive reflection in the next 10 days, and you will make even more progress by the end of your first 100 days.

10 Are you having fun?

A new role is a serious milestone in the career of an ambitious executive. But all work and no fun make for an overly serious approach to work and life – and nobody wants to work for someone too serious/too dull! Start planning your 'End of my First 100 Days' celebration. You can organise a fun social event with your team to celebrate the milestone and thank them for welcoming you, and praise them for all their efforts to date.

2 Write your 10-day 'to-do' list

As mentioned in Chapter 2 there is a significant difference between a 'plan' and a 'to-do' list. So far, it's been all about the plan but, at day 90, I think the smartest thing you can do is be very focused and – using your First 100 Days Plan as the backdrop – simply write a to-do list of all the things you are going to tightly focus on in the next 10 days, to bring your First 100 Days journey to an effective and successful close.

what are the urgent and important priorities for the next 10 days?

With your First 100 Days desired outcomes as the backdrop, think about how you can best focus your time in the next 10 days in relation to your desired outcomes on:

- transition maker
- unique contributor
- content learner
- business achiever
- team builder
- communications provider
- relationship builder
- value adder
- culture navigator
- market player.

If it feels too overwhelming to think about all 10 outcomes, then be practical and realistic and simply focus on one or two of your key desired outcomes. Then write a list of tasks that can be completed by day 100, taking into account who can help you.

3 Ask for feedback

Someone once said that the problem with feedback is that no one really wants to give it and no one really wants to receive it! At First100™ we always say 'It is better to know' and, for sure, in the context of the first 100 days, it is better to know sooner rather than later, if there is a leadership style issue or any unwitting cultural gaffes taking place that are preventing stakeholder relationship building and performance acceleration.

You need to realise that, as soon as you become the boss, you stop hearing the truth about what is really going on around you.

'you are doing a great job' is not feedback – it may not even be true!

Usually, people only want to please the boss, and give him or her good news. Very often, it is because the boss reacts with anger – even shooting the messenger – if he or she hears bad news … so be careful how, as the boss, you react to bad news – or you will never ever hear it again!

Typically, in the first 100 days, unless you go out of your way to gather information, feedback from your boss stays at surface-level only – 'You're doing a great job, just keep going'. This is a lazy 'throw away' line that people use when they haven't thought it through, and think that you are simply looking for encouragement rather than actual feedback. Unfortunately, there is rarely a culture of healthy feedback-giving in corporations, so your boss will often not be comfortable or able to give you useful feedback. Plus, your boss is the person who hired you, so he or she has too much of a vested interest in your success and will be incentivised to see all the positives in you rather than any weaknesses at this stage. You need to appreciate that your boss will still be in the mode of justifying their hiring decision to their own boss. It would be more mature and grounded of you to accept this dynamic, and to find other ways to get real feedback on your first 100 days.

You need to make a very conscious effort to get real feedback. Don't ask in such a way that people think you are looking for reassurance. Ask in a way that demonstrates you truly are looking for honest feedback.

- Ask for feedback formally, via company 360 Degree Performance Appraisals.

- Ask for feedback informally; ask people who you think will tell you the truth, and let them know that you are okay with anything they say and that you will not shoot the messenger.

- Check if more than one person is telling you the same thing – if the message is consistent, then it's probably true (or the perception is true).

- As soon as someone gives you feedback, whether you agree with what they are saying or not, always say, 'thank you' and (if you can handle it!) say, 'can you tell me more'. Instead of being defensive, move into exploratory/curiousity mode to uncover what they are really trying to convey. Treat honest feedback like a gift and don't take it personally if you don't like what you hear. Feedback is about your leadership behaviour or skills, which are things that you can change.

- Be alert, use active listening to hear what people are really saying. For example, what are they saying 'above the surface' versus what they really mean 'below the surface'? It is 100 per cent true that actions speak louder than words, so feel free to disregard what people are saying and observe instead what people are doing.

● Work with an independent coach whose job is to help you to reduce your blind spots.

don't ask for reassurance, ask for feedback

My suggestion is that you should 'make a virtue' of gathering feedback after your first 90 days. Hire an external independent third party such as a First100™ Coach to run your @ 90 days feedback exercise encompassing: upwards (your boss), at level (two to four peers), below level (three to five direct reports) and any other important role stakeholders (e.g. customer).

The very act of conducting a formal @ 90 day feedback exercise will signal to your stakeholders and team that you are interested in monitoring your progress. This openness is a major differentiating leadership win in itself, and your stakeholders will be very impressed by your willingness to get early feedback and to treat it seriously. Naturally, the bigger prize should also be in actually getting the feedback and capitalising on it to inform you of perceptions, to reduce your blind spots and increase your chances of success in this organisation within the first 100 days and first 12 months.

The following is a suggested effective template that can be used by a third party to conduct a useful 360 degree exercise with your team (e.g. all your direct reports), your peers (two or three only) and your key upward stakeholders (e.g. your boss, and your boss's boss) and externals (two or three only – for example your key customers).

You can go beyond a '360 view' to conduct what has become known as a '450' by also taking time out for self-reflection, to reduce blind spots. This is best done with the help of a third-party professional executive coach, because it is hard for us to step outside ourselves and spot our own self-sabotaging behaviour without the expert help of another person.

As you will see in the @ 90 day feedback exercise form, I deliberately keep the questions very simple and very open-ended. I want you to get real feedback, by allowing your stakeholders the freedom to express their views and not be hampered by a predetermined set of leading close-ended questions or a checklist. This is not the usual corporate box-ticking performance appraisal exercise, this is about taking an opportunity to really hear free unfettered undiluted views from others. Typically, of course, others will self-edit their feedback anyway out of self-preservation – particularly in the case of your team members! – because they don't know you well enough yet to trust how you might respond to very candid feedback. This is why you need your third-party professional to read between the lines, and help you hear what was said and sometimes – more interestingly! – what was left unsaid, and what can be implied from this.

@ 90 day feedback exercise
Stakeholder feedback form

SECTION 1 WHAT IS YOUR OVERALL IMPRESSION OF HIS/HER LEADERSHIP STYLE AND IMPACT TO DATE?

SECTION 2 LEADERSHIP SKILL	Please rank the recently appointed leader's performance as high, medium or low. Please also provide comments and examples to underpin your ranking.

▶

On vision and strategy – *Sets a clear direction*	
On people and teams – *Brings people with him/her*	
On results and deliverables – *Gets right results*	

SECTION 3 WHAT SUGGESTIONS/TIPS CAN YOU OFFER THE RECENTLY APPOINTED LEADER FOR MOVING FORWARD?

4 Take time out for self-reflection

I am not your king or prime minister but I am going to grant you a half-day off from the routine of your day-to-day office. You have worked hard for the past 90 days, and the smartest thing you could do now is take up to three hours off from your usual working day to leave the office, and sit in a pleasant café on your own and think back on your whole transition – from the preparation stage to now; what worked, what didn't, how you stacked up as a person, as a leader during the last 90 days.

- What is your personal highlight?
- What was your lowest moment?

- How did you recover from knock-backs?
- Who really helped you since you joined?
- What are your biggest lessons learned?
- What would you do differently, if you could do it all over again?

Self-reflection is not an indulgence, it is crucial in a fast-paced world. Everything moves so fast these days, and decisions are taken very quickly – often with little time to reflect back on the consequences of those decisions, and to learn the lessons.

are you proud of you?

The very concept of taking time out for 'self-reflection' may be an alien one, but remember that, if you want to continue to grow as a leader, then you need to apply new techniques and methods to find the angles and the self-growth opportunities; the ability to take time out of your day, step back and simply be on your own and reflect on your own progress.

5 Critical success factors for the final 10 days: day 90–100

The following is a summary heads up on what you should be thinking about in your final 10 days.

CROSS THE FINISH LINE

I truly believe 'a good start is half the work' but equally important is a good finish. Being a completer-finisher on your First 100 Days journey will give you an immense feeling of satisfaction but will also motivate you to start your new journey to the end of the next 12 months. You have 10 days left, use them effectively to wrap up, tidy up and speed up any remaining tasks that should be completed by the end of your first 100 days. You are on the home stretch and these next 10 days are the final hurdle. After all of your hard work, it is important to stay focused and not lose sight of your goal. Your first 100 days will have an impact for the next 12 months and beyond so make sure you close out your first 100 days as strongly and enthusiastically as you started them. You will reap the long-term rewards.

TAKE 'TIME OUT'

Take some time to reflect on what's worked and what hasn't. Take time to celebrate what has worked and the progress you have made. It's time to give yourself a healthy dose of recognition of what you've achieved to date. It's time to feel really good about yourself and value your efforts and progress. Not only will this have a long-term effect of well-being but it will show your team the value you place on yourself and, in turn, on them. You will come back to the realities of your fast-paced environment feeling refreshed and renewed by celebrating your achievements to date and taking a little time out to pause and bask in the results.

LEARN FROM YOUR MISTAKES

Having gathered feedback from others and taken some time out for self-reflection, consider what you would have done differently. Accept that there's no failure, just feedback. If something went wrong, or if you feel you made a mistake in your first 100 days, accept that as useful feedback. It just wasn't the right approach. Try another. Do not give yourself a hard time. Turn what went wrong into a positive of what can be done right in the future.

First100™ client case study continued

JOHN, NEWLY APPOINTED GLOBAL HEAD OF SALES FOR PREMIUM SERVICES, ABC BANK

'I have finished my first 100 days, now what?!'

As John waited for his First100™ Coach to turn up for his final 'First 100 Days' session, he reflected back on the last three to four months. It had been quite a rollercoaster of emotions from the high of getting the job to the low point of realising his team were not up to standard. What really stood out for him, however, was the emotional relief he felt once he had developed his First 100 Days Plan. Looking back, John acknowledged that this was the moment when he felt in control for the first time. Perhaps he needed another 100-day plan to see him through the next three months?

Coach notes

John, you need to shift gears now. Yes, your First 100 Days Plan has served you well. But it is over, and you cannot be short-termist and simply lurch from 100 days to 100 days. You need close out your First 100 Days Plan, draw a line under it – and then think about a new longer-term plan. Your next critical moment of judgement will be when you have been in your role for a total of 12 months. When you have been in your role for a year, this is the time when your added value will come under even more scrutiny – especially from any would-be detractors and critics. Get ahead of that by writing what I call your 'Second Act' Plan. Take all the lessons you have learned about the importance of having a plan, starting with the end in mind, punctuating the plan with key milestones, and reviewing progress at those milestones – but focus on an 8- to 9-month 'Second Act' Plan that takes you from here to the end of your first 12 months.

Focus on the next 8–9 months' view, and craft the desired outcomes you want to achieve by the end of your first 12 months in the role. But … before you do that, let's finish up your first 100 days. Let's acknowledge that it has come to an end, let's acknowledge the lessons learned. What have you done well? What have you done not so well? How do you rate your own performance? How do your team and stakeholders rate your performance?

Close out your plan, record achievements and lessons learned, and then move on to your second act.

Looking back, John felt that having a structured First 100 Days Plan was absolutely critical to his self-management, but he now also realised that his biggest leadership skill and personal growth had been in the area of emotional intelligence. John could see more clearly, now, how nervous he had been at the beginning of his role, and how he had suffered a confidence dip. If he hadn't had the First 100 Days Plan, or the support of his First100™ Coach, John realised that he wouldn't have made so much progress – because, by being better able to manage the emotional life of his job, he suffered less stress, tackled challenges better, made good decisions and performed at his peak, despite all the ambiguity and difficulties inherent in his leadership tasks.

Indeed, John was surprised at how much he had achieved, given how impossible the task seemed at the start. John's boss was extremely impressed with him, and wanted to expand John's area of responsibility to include a new strategic global internal project regarding the importance of emerging markets and a potential restructure of the whole company. John knew that the outcome of this strategic review would, ultimately, impact him in his career and he was pleased to be so in control of his existing role that he could participate on the project that ultimately would shape his own future career at the company. John confided in the colleague who put him in touch with the First100™ Coach, 'Getting the first 100 days right has been a turning point, not just for this role, but I realise now that it has been a turning point in my leadership career.'

7

End

- Close out your First 100 Days Plan
- Record achievements and capture lessons learned
- Communicate First 100 Days success to stakeholders
- Celebrate with your team
- Consider your 'Second Act'

1 Close out your First 100 Days Plan

In the same way that some people don't like to let go of their previous role when they get a new job, some people don't like to let go of their First 100 Days Plan and process! I had one client who elongated his First 100 Days Plan to last for six months! He was still talking about his First 100 Days Plan long after his first 100 days were over. This only **your first 100 days are over; draw a line under it and move on** will make you look foolish, so, when the literal first 100 days of your new leadership appointment has passed, it is time to stop talking about your First 100 Days Plan. It is over, so draw a line under it and move on to your 'Second Act'– see the final section!

2 Record achievements and capture lessons learned

Consider the First 100 Days Plan as a javelin throw. At the time, you set out a number of outcomes to be achieved – then, inevitably, organisation life and market dynamics got in the way.

Not everybody completes everything that they set out to achieve in their plan. But let's hope you followed the instructions, and made it most of the way there. So, now is the time to take stock, record your achievements and think about next steps.

- Are your two-year strategic aspirations on track?
- Did you achieve some/most/all of your desired outcomes by the end of the first 100 days?

- What are the lessons learned about: you as a leader, the role, the organisation, the market?
- What are your proposed next steps?

I suggest you use the following template for inspiration, and make a 'First 100 Days' presentation to your boss/board/role stakeholders. Be inclusive about the efforts of your team, and remember to include discussion about 'our' achievements versus highlighting only 'my' achievements.

Don't miss the timing and opportunity to ask for more budget and more resources. If you can demonstrate that you had a great first 100 days, then now is the time to ask your stakeholders (your 'investors') to back you further. One success leads to another. If you have a great first 100 days, then you will be in a better position to get more resources (people, time, money). If you get more resources, then you are more likely to be successful going forward.

one success leads to another

RECORD OF MY LEADERSHIP ACHIEVEMENTS *@ THE END OF THE FIRST 100 DAYS*	
At macro level On vision and strategy On people and teams On results and deliverables	
At micro level Versus each of my 'First 100 Days' 10 desired outcomes	

Key lessons learned	
Proposed next steps	
Request for extra budget and people	

3 Communicate First 100 Days success to stakeholders

Use your record of achievements to communicate your First 100 Days success to your stakeholders. All along, I have used the 'journey' metaphor to describe your First 100 Days transition, and you need to make sure you are bringing everybody with you on this journey – or that they catch up with where you are at the end of your First 100 Days journey. Whether or not you have formally presented your First 100 Days Plan to stakeholders, you can still use the 'end of the first 100 days' marker to talk about what you have achieved.

communication, communication, communication

Remember, there are no medals for modesty in the business world! This is the point where you get to take pride in your success and relay to your key stakeholders the accelerated progress you have made in a relatively short period of time. Do not underestimate the importance of sharing what you have done. You won't want to come across as arrogant, but you do need to ensure it is well communicated and your achievements are given due recognition. The plan and the results themselves will impress but so will the enthusiasm and confidence with which you are sharing them. This also gives you the opportunity to recognise your team and to thank your stakeholders for helping you achieve the right results. Remember, this is about joint success and bringing people with you at all levels and isn't a solo run.

Everyone likes good news and usually we don't hear or commemorate the 'good stuff' often enough. You've worked hard to get to this point, so work hard to communicate the successes effectively too.

4 Celebrate with your team

As a leader, you need to look constantly for opportunities to build the morale of your followers, and the end of your first 100 days as their new leader is as good an excuse for celebration as any! You need to realise and acknowledge that your team have been through a challenging transition of their own – the challenging transition of having a new boss! Their excitement and their anxiety about you as their new leader started long before you arrived, and continued after you arrived:

- Who are you, why were you chosen?
- Why should we be led by you?
- Can I trust you?
- Will I keep my job?
- Are you a reasonable boss?
- Can you build a great team?
- Have you made a difference?
- Am I proud to be on your team?

So, in acknowledgement of the transition that all of you have been through – in the first 100 days, and prior – now is the time to celebrate the end of the First 100 Days milestone. My suggestion is that you schedule a social event and my additional suggestion is that you foot the bill from your own personal funds. You are paid more than everyone else on your team, they work hard for you and my advice is that you should be generous with your team. You will get a return on the investment in terms of their loyalty, and their generosity of hard work back to you. It is appropriate now to deepen the relationship bond with your team and, if they know that you have paid from your own salary, then they will appreciate you and the event even more. Your people are your best asset, and you need to continue to invest in and nurture that asset to maximise its potential.

Your team will have helped you to achieve your First 100 Days Plan. By involving them in your journey, it will have motivated them. Your followers want to feel part of your plan. By celebrating its success, the motivational factor becomes tenfold. It has been widely reported that 'the sense of making progress' is the number-one motivator to building and maintaining a high-performing team. Acknowledge the progress made as a newly formed team and mark the occasion with a celebration.

This needs to be a fun night out, so, if you do coincide it with a team meeting, then when the work is done, put the paperwork away, put the stresses away, just relax and have fun, and enjoy getting to know your co-workers. Take this as an opportunity to let them get to you know you as well, as a person and not just their boss. The more your team can relate to you, the better.

5 Consider your 'Second Act'

In my experience, there are typically two key moments of judgement of the newly appointed executive:

- the end of the first 100 days;
- the end of the first 12 months.

If you are reading this book, and applying the principles, then it is more likely that you are the one driving the desire for judgement and approval from your boss, peers and team by the end of your first 100 days. However, at the end of your first year in the role – with or without any drive on your part – the people around you will automatically start making a judgement on you. If you don't pay attention to the 'one-year' milestone, you may find that all your efforts back in your first 100 days are rewritten by others as merely good early PR moves. It may seem like an odd thing to say but, in order to maintain the success of your first 100 days, you will need to pay specific attention to how you are viewed at the end of your first 12 months in the role. For example, US President Obama was deemed to have had a very successful first 100 days, but his detractors had a field day at the 12-month mark and, as such, his first 100 days are no longer perceived as such a great success after all.

So now it is time to close out your First 100 Days Plan and focus on a longer-term 'Second Act' Plan, i.e. now focus on what you want to have achieved by your second moment of judgement. First100™ clients are often so pleased with the success of their first 100 days that they think they should have another 100-day plan, but having a series of 100-day sprints is not something I would advise. My suggestion is to sprint in your first 100 days and run a marathon in your next nine months to take you successfully to the end of your first year.

shift from sprint to marathon

My thoughts on the 'Second Act' are worthy of another book(!) but, in brief, you need to think about it as a 'renew and resurge'.

RENEW

Write a new plan: your 'Second Act' Plan that will take you forward to the end of your first 12 months. Your desired outcomes are focused on what you want to have achieved by end of the first 12 months. Your new milestones will be quarterly (not monthly): i.e. end of 6 months, end of 9 months, end of 12 months.

RESURGE

You need a resurge of effort and activity that will take you through the next nine months. I call it the 3 Rs:

- **Renew** your narrative: what is your new story, the new narrative that you can use to excite and enthuse your team and stakeholders for the next phase of the journey?
- **Remotivate** your team: what else can you do to motivate your people to keep working hard?
- **Refocus** on results: you have just delivered some great results in your first 100 days but, of course, the results need to keep on coming(!), so think about the key results that you need to deliver at the end of your first 12 months.

So, that's it. Your first 100 days are over, you have achieved maximum impact, and now it is time to focus on your 'Second Act'.

Final words

I hope that, by now, you feel very comfortable in your new 'role skin'.

Your first 100 days set the tone for who you are as a leader and what you want to achieve with your new role. It is the beginning phase of what will, ultimately, become your complete leadership role legacy, and a good start bodes well for a strong and effective whole role legacy.

With the help of the insights and approaches in this book, you have successfully accelerated your performance and made maximum leadership impact that will not just positively affect your first 100 days in this role, but will equip you for having maximum leadership success during the first 12 months and your whole role tenure and beyond. The coaching in this book will, hopefully, have enabled the vital processes of leadership to be awakened in you, and can be a catalyst for your leadership growth going forward.

The content in this book can act as a catalyst for long-term leadership skills transformation, which includes:

● increased confidence;
● better decision making;
● growth in emotional intelligence;
● more effectiveness at structured planning and managing uncertainty;
● greater ability to set a clear direction and motivate others to follow.

By applying the concepts in this book, you can continue to enjoy longer-term leadership transformational benefits, as you become

be the best leader you can be

more skilled and more experienced on putting the concepts to work at whatever stage you are at in your role appointment lifecycle.

As a final note, I would urge you to be the best leader you can be.

At its core, this book is all about helping you to improve the quality of your leadership skills – with particular emphasis on the beginning of a new role as a moment of need that attracts your attention and appetite for learning. We need to get your attention, because we need our leaders to be even better than before. Some commentators say that we have suffered an economic crisis – but I believe it is more accurate to say that we suffered a leadership crisis and that the global economic meltdown is merely symptomatic. As the world comes to terms with the financial meltdown just endured, our business leaders need to emerge better and stronger. Our business leaders need to try harder, to take more responsibility, to deliver better outcomes faster. We need to see the emergence of a new breed of senior executive who will take their role seriously from the beginning, create structure out of chaos, lead by example, motivate their teams to deliver on missions that will strengthen their organisations, create stability and help maintain jobs and boost the economy.

For newly appointed senior leaders everywhere, now is your time. This is your call to action. We are looking to you to bring us forward. You can play a very personal role in improving the quality of leadership in the world by stepping up in your role, in your organisation, by having a great first 100 days, and then taking your team and people ever further forward in the months and years ahead.

Thank you for reading this book, and good luck.

Index

READ ON

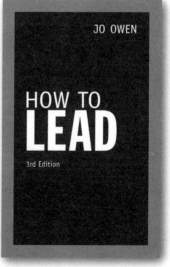